The Economic Person

The Economic Person

Acting and Analyzing

Peter L. Danner

ROWMAN & LITTLEFIELD PUBLISHERS, INC.
Lanham • Boulder • New York • Oxford

ROWMAN & LITTLEFIELD PUBLISHERS, INC.

Published in the United States of America
by Rowman & Littlefield Publishers, Inc.
4720 Boston Way, Lanham, Maryland 20706
www.rowmanlittlefield.com

12 Hid's Copse Road
Cumnor Hill, Oxford OX2 9JJ, England

British Library Cataloguing in Publication Information Available

Library of Congress Cataloging-in-Publication Data

Danner, Peter L.
    The economic person : acting and analyzing / Peter L. Danner.
        p. cm.
    Includes bibliographical references and index.
    ISBN 0-7425-1306-8 (alk. paper) — ISBN 0-7425-1307-6 (pbk. : alk. paper)
    1. Economic man. 2. Economics—Philosophy. 3. Economics—History. I. Title.

    HB72 .D232 2002
    330.1—dc21

                                                                    2001041690

Printed in the United States of America

♾TM The paper used in this publication meets the minimum requirements of American
National Standard for Information Sciences—Permanence of Paper for Printed Library
Materials, ANSI/NISO Z.39.48-1992.

Contents

Preface

The economic person is both practitioner and scientist, the former because of the need to survive and the latter because of the need to understand. As economic agents, men and women for their material needs naturally engaged in economic activities for many millennia long before they thought it necessary to analyze the principles of what they practiced. But as local economies blended into national and then international economies, economic scholars and savants began to analyze these activities as collective phenomena, whether domestic, national, and international trade is waxing or waning; prices and wages increasing or declining; capital values gaining or losing; and how they all interrelate in affecting the price index, money supply, employment, national income, and so forth. Besides analyzing these trends, professional economists must also gather and correlate the information needed to make these never-ending evaluations, which in turn contribute to the economic milieu of constant change.

Consequently, economists must be as continuously on tap to predict the economic climate as meteorologists must be to forecast the weather. The difference is that neither weather forecasts nor people's response to them will change the weather, while economic predictions do tend to affect what they predict, either corroborating or making them worse. That is, unlike meteorologists who study weather changes isolated from people's responses to them, economists study activities that people must actively engage in for both their survival and gratification. Therefore, whatever economists' professional analyses and predictions may be, persons react to them and in turn cause them to change. To repeat, economic persons engage in—and have for millennia engaged in—the economic activity that economic scientists only relatively recently have begun to analyze in a scientific way.

This results in a difference in how the economic person, as economic subject and as practitioner, is perceived. As the subject of economic science and
analysis, human beings tend to lose their distinctiveness as individual persons
and are seen simply as impersonal economic agents, placing acts that become
the subject of economic analysis. Such is the implication of *homo economicus*. By contrast the concept of the 'economic person' is of a fully fledged and
morally responsible human being, who may be viewed as analyzing and
studying economics but mainly as *doing economics.*

That is, the economic person as doing economics—buying and selling, employed and employing, borrowing and lending, innovating and investing—
engages in activities necessitated by the human condition as an *embodied
spirit.* While a self-knowing and self-acting spirit, the human person can survive physically and place acts that relate him or her to the material universe
and to other human persons by way of the materiality of the body's physical
acts. Moreover, material things, while necessary for survival, are almost
never found usable just for the taking but must be processed and marketed.
Everyone, therefore, must engage in economic activity, must *do economics,*
not alone but with other persons. In short, what one person does affects what
others do or can do. Economic praxis, therefore, is both necessary and social,
and the economic person, as distinguished from the abstract *homo economicus*, must act in concert with other persons and is morally responsible for
his/her actions.

As a social being, the economic person must be honest and just in his or
her economic dealings and generate a sense of trust in fellow workers, em-
ployers, customers, and the like. This is fundamental to the whole purpose of
gaining from economic actions, relations, and transactions; that is, basic to all
economic production and exchanges is the desire by each party to gain, to realize a greater benefit from surrendering some good, be it money, time, or effort. Economic gaining, however, cannot be unilateral. Buyers and sellers
each must be willing to sacrifice some good in expectation of gaining a more
preferred good. It took no economist to figure out that the very essence of
every economic act is the mutual exchange of one's good for something more
desired, and that this is the very engine of economic growth.

Indeed, economic growth and continuing economic relations require a relatively permanent condition of mutual trust among the transactors. Called
credit, which is simply the Latin for "he or she believes or trusts," it is the
fundamental glue in every economic exchange. Converted from the act of
trusting to the general condition of being trustworthy and actually trusted,
credit has become the transglobal economic good and as such is essential for
economic gain and thus economic growth. Cro-Magnon in his tribal and in-
tertribal dealings was as aware of this as was Henry Ford in selling his
"flivvers": so much down and so much per month. Indeed, economic trust

will tap into other virtues: honesty, justice, control of sensual appetites, even fortitude in meeting one's obligations, and the social need to cooperate with others. This sense of needing certain basic virtues, however, is often lost in the fact that economic acts are placed in a vast, interrelated and constantly changing network of exchange relationships.

The rationality of acting in such a milieu is to choose to buy or sell, to produce or not, or to save or to invest depending on the prices charged and other costs. Since any price or system of prices in this complex influences other prices and they in turn others, all prices are constantly changing—even though indiscernibly—as the many factors affecting them change. (Thus in modern economies, price statistics must be gathered daily, price changes analyzed regularly, and market influences studied continuously, none of which was deemed necessary or possible three centuries ago.) But more to the point, individual economic acts must be placed in a vast interconnecting and ever-changing series of acts. This means that what one person buys, sells, spends, or saves necessarily has an effect, although microscopic, on the whole economic process. Because of these interpersonal circumstances, every person's action affects every other person, some perceptibly, most not. That is, even though the private and personal is lost in the complexities of the whole, the economy does establish a *moral context:* individual acts affect other people and their actions and thus can be judged useful or wasteful, honest or dishonest, just or unjust, greedy or generous, and, therefore, morally good or bad.

Consequently, the economic acts of the economic practitioner, as distinct from those of the economic analyst, must be judged by two criteria: economic morality and economic rationality. As moral, economic acts can be judged honest, cooperative, and just. As rational, they must seem to improve one's functional condition; they must be gainful. Inevitably these two principles will seem to clash in particular cases. More frequently economic rationality will tend to make more sense than economic morality. But that may be more illusion than reality. For one easy-to-see example: an unjust wage policy that beefs up profits in the short run may motivate good workers to quit in the long run.

At the same time it must be admitted that what is both the efficient and just wage will never finally be realized: efficiency and justice seem to tilt endlessly at each other. The tension between the two principles, however, may in the long run work toward what is best for all concerned; that is, in the dynamics of daily business the efficiency and justice of a given policy can always be improved. In one sense this present study, therefore, hopes that exploring personalist principles as they relate both to economic rationality and to morality will be of some help in removing some of the dissidence that people see between the two. A brief review of these may be helpful in focusing the subsequent analyses.

First, the principles of *economic rationality*. What is most obvious is that the economic agent's material acting and surviving needs must become specific as wants for particular goods and services, which in turn must be produced and brought to market. This implies a *social process:* individuals collaborating to make available the goods and services other people need and want. Obviously, therefore, economic products as well as individuals' productive services and contributions are prized in a general way for their exchange values, usually expressed as prices. Since almost everything is *priced,* an individual gains, or improves his or her well-being, by paying the prices for what others are selling. In turn, *homo economicus* by contributing to producing and sharing in gain from sales to others, is assumed to act out of *self-interest*, following the rule of pricing set by supply and demand forces in *impersonal markets*. In all of this a basic economic rationality rules that is secular and this-worldly and, therefore, *a-moral,* but not of itself immoral. Economic rationality, what the economic professional prescribes, therefore, has as its goal the laudable purpose that people may live as well physically as possible in this present world and life.

Economic morality is no less this-worldly but with an all-important difference. It includes all the features of economic rationality: material needing and wanting, productive collaborating, monetary rewarding through the marketing process, and gaining material goods, all of which are motivated by self-interest. Virtuous living, therefore, does not argue for returning to the cave nor seeking some state of moral El Dorado. Economic morality does, however, differ from economic rationality in one important dimension: it is rational in terms of persons' *supraphysical* purposes and for many an *ultramundane* destiny. Furthermore, economic persons are naturally by conception and birth *other-related and social.* This requires sharing the goods of nature and of the economy, as well as collaborating with others to produce the goods and services people need and want. From these common needs, people can form *true economic community,* and from these common needs, also, economic self-interest can contain many degrees of *altruism,* that is, concern for others' well-being. Monetary values, too, are not just means of exchange but can embody *personal values,* especially that of *utility.* They in turn, therefore, can reflect one's personal goals, those ultimate goods as values worth striving for. All adds up to an important sense of *personal freedom* and *responsibility* for what one does and seeks of the goods of this world. Economic goals, while respected for themselves and sought on their own merit, should be valued mainly as means toward an economic person's communal functions and one's ultimate destiny as a person.

In summary, economics as science is empirical and mathematical. Its axioms and laws are preceptive—instructive of the rational way to devise, produce, and trade material goods and services. It deals with quantified, hence abstract, realities: markets and market movements, planes of living, flows of trade, financial forces, rates of inflation, and so forth. Economics as praxis is no less governed by the same precepts but in a more concrete manner: this steamfitter job, a box of Wheaties, your checking account, and insurance policies. In addition, as the activity of human persons, it is governed by normative standards of conduct. While economic science and economic praxis can be differentiated, ideally, the economic analyst should be wary of formulating concepts to conflict with ethical norms, and the ethicist should be conscious of the material context in which economic aspirations and acts are placed.

It cannot be stressed too much, therefore, that economic science and economic praxis are distinct but necessarily related. Economic science perceives economic activities abstractly as demand and supply, production and markets, innovations and investments, debts and loans, profits and losses, and the rest, all abstracted from the actual human activity of satisfying wants and needs in order to concentrate on and illustrate their interactive effects. It justifies, therefore, perceiving the economy abstractly as a system that runs by its own logic and on its inner energy. On the other hand, no matter how elaborate the scientific system that modern economists describe, such economists cannot ignore the nitty-gritty of daily human economic relating, wanting, and acting. Moreover, even to keep its abstract mechanism up to date, economists not only must acknowledge the actual changes taking place in the system itself, e.g., the revolution in women's economic roles, but must be aware of the implications of moral critique as it responds to ever changing circumstances. It is this that justifies examining some of the basic economic principles from the insights of a personalist philosophy.

I must confess that I came to these convictions relatively late in my professional career, although it began with a thorough grounding in philosophy. It illustrates that ancient but sad dictum, "So soon old, so late smart!" In a life and career that never flagged into ennui, what with addressing family concerns, academic interests and department business, Association for Social Economics' activities, private consulting, and the like, I was able to squeeze out little time for writing.

However, my first book, begun in 1965 on a year's study grant in France from the Society for Values in Education, was published in 1980. *An Ethics for the Affluent* was intended for undergraduates: "Its subject is ethics as applied in economic relations, and its orientation is personalist. . . . The moral problems and issues encountered in business will be treated here as auxiliary and illustrative to the central concern for personal moral development." The book was frankly functional in purpose and I enjoyed teaching it despite its defects. *Getting and Spending*, coming fourteen years later, went further toward formulating the "fundamental attitude of economic morality, a consistent and coherent guide of economic and business conduct, blended from both moral and economic principles of action. . . . (It) starts from a personalist conception of men and women and views the economy and economic acts as essentially social."

The present work, more theoretical in intent, digs deeper into the meaning and functions of the personalist nature of men and women as the bedrock moral criterion of economic acts. Thus it insists on persons' economic proclivities long before professional economics was devised or conceptualized. In fact, it asserts that the ultimate criteria of economic science are people's natural inclinations to conceive, produce, and trade material goods and services for human use and benefit. For humans there is no escape: the economic person is as fundamental and essential as the loving and knowing person. Indeed this concept plumbs the innermost necessity of both economic praxis and analysis. Beyond the problems economic ethics poses and the nitty-gritty of actual getting and spending, analysis of the human person as an economic person gets to the essential nature of human needing and thus to the economics of generating material goods and services for human use. In so doing, the book probes a few of the basic economic principles in terms of their illuminating the materiality of human persons and their natural activities as economic practitioners.

A moment's pause to think of one's household, one's city, the country, and the world and to picture the flow of traffic, the surge of people coming and going, the vast towers of commerce and finance, and the elaborate processes of construction and production, all involving millions and billions of people from the dense canyons of New York to the tundra towns of Siberia, reveals persons of every ethnicity, color, and culture all busily engaged in economic praxis and a few also in economic analysis. While Wordsworth complained that in getting and spending we lay waste our lives, the one basic fact is that we are primarily spirits needing to know and to love but spirits, nevertheless, who need and must work through bodies to create from the powers and raw materials of the universe the beautiful as well as the useful things for living.

This means, consequently, that all the principles that guide this activity, like seeking to improve one's well-being by giving up something for something more desired, like needing to work with and for others to get what one wants, like striving to derive the most good or value from things we do have, and above all like working, playing, learning with, and loving others in a vast common good, all rationally and ideally work toward a common goal of improving how people live. The economic goal is not the noblest but it is a fundamentally good and necessary one.

This, in turn, implies my conviction that the economic good and the moral good are compatible in theory and workable in practice. This conclusion I gradually reached in the course of an education which ranged over literature, philosophy, history, moral theology, and economic theory. From a galaxy of wonderful teachers, three, however, stand out as pertinent to the present work. Bernard W. Dempsey, S.J., my mentor at St. Louis University, was the first to resolve conflicts between fundamental ethical and economic principles and to introduce me to the economic wisdom of Joseph A. Schumpeter, his own mentor at Harvard. Next, I owe much to Theo Suranyi-Unger of Syracuse University, who guided me toward an understanding of Adam Smith's social insights. Finally, the *Personalism* of Emmanuel Mounier, whom I never met, left a lasting impression that then was sparked to exciting significance by the 1993 lecture of John F. Kavanaugh, S.J., at Marquette University and his subsequent monograph, *Recovery of Personhood: An Ethics After Post-Modernism.* It was that which started the process of perceiving a personalist theme in my teaching of economic principles and the reading of the history of economic thought.

This reading revealed that early scholars perceived economics as mainly the praxis of persons, emphasizing their obligations to share their bounty, to use it prudently and lawfully, and to lend and trade it justly. As, however, local and regional economies grew into national economies, scholars like Smith, Ricardo, Menger, Marshall, and Keynes gradually formulated a body of principles that could be perceived abstractly as a set of dynamic relationships and that inevitably reflected the empirical, a-moral, and secular Zeitgeist of the nineteenth century. Inevitably this demoted *homo economicus* to a mere economic agent without moral principles. Nevertheless, the older tradition continued of seeing religious, philosophical, social, and humanistic factors influencing people's economic actions. It inevitably suggests examining the economic agent as a self-knowing but embodied spirit. This melding of the material and spiritual, the empirical and the metaphysical, suggests the need to reexamine some basic economic principles.

Economic *scarcity*, therefore, is reinterpreted as the need for a pricing technique to work up and share the universe's bountiful resources. Economic values, expressed mainly as prices, are then analyzed as the empirical means by which personal and moral values are espoused and value hierarchies fashioned. Personal *gain seeking,* then, is analyzed as the economy's drive, distinct from but like the sense appetites necessary to existence and prone to excess. Next, economic institutions are perceived as requiring both a person's sense of community and an individual's self-interest. Finally, the three social values of liberty, equality, and fraternity are shown to comprise the social/political/economic common good, which in turn requires economic competition, collaboration, and government mediation. Last of all, as with natural and human coalescence, self-interest melds with altruism (other-interest) to generate economic well-being. All told, therefore, this interworking of philosophic and economic thought by way of rethinking and reworking past papers and articles has produced *The Economic Person: Acting and Analyzing.*

Indeed the personalist development of chapters 5 through 9 grew out of earlier papers into which personalist insights generated extensive modifications and a total recasting. Thus chapter 5, "Personalism and Scarcity," grew out of my totally reworked article "Personalism and the Problem of Scarcity" which appeared in the *Forum for Social Economics,* Fall 1995. Chapter 6, "Personal and Economic Values," was also a complete rewriting of my article, "Personalism, Values, and Economic Values," which was included in the October 1982 issue of the *Review of Social Economy.* Chapter 7, "Personalism and Gain Seeking," is also an extensive recasting and rewriting of an earlier article which appeared as "Gain-Seeking: the Econo-Moral Nexus" in *Social Economics: Premises, Findings, and Policies,* edited by Edward J. O'Boyle (London: Routledge, 1996). Chapter 8, "Personalism and Economic Community," again was developed and rewritten from my article "The Moral Foundations of Community" in the December 1984 issue of the *Review of Social Economy.* Chapter 9, "Personalism and Common Good," grew out of and was pervasively modified from "The Person and the Social Economy: Needs, Values, and Principles," a chapter in *The Social Economics of Human Material Need,* edited by John B. Davis and Edward J. O'Boyle (Carbondale, Ill.: Southern Illinois University Press, 1994). Finally, chapter 10, "Economic Persons in Action," grew from the very process of interpreting these earlier analyses of basic economic concepts and principles from a more thorough personalist perspective. This process, however, does not lessen in any way my gratitude to the editors of the *Review* and the *Forum,* to Routledge, and the Southern Illinois University Press for publishing these earlier essays.

My gratitude is heartfelt also for my colleagues in the Association for Social Economics: Steve Worland, Arnold McKee, John Davis, Doug Booth, Ed O'Boyle, Pat Welch, Tom Bausch, Steve Pressman, Warren Samuels, and others for their critiques, advice, and encouragement. Among these also should be included other Marquette colleagues like the Jesuit Fathers Robert Lambeck, Thomas Caldwell, and William Kidd, and the always willing and competent University staff people like Ann Mallinger, Thomas Wicker, Megan Maloney, Sue Fligor, April Fleischmann, Gene Prey, Ramon Luzarraga, and, most especially, Debbie Tadych. I am also greatly indebted to Román Jimenez and John Tadych Jr. for their technical support, to my son Larry Danner, and to the staff people at Milwaukee PC for calming my nerves and coaching me to reasonable competence in use of a contemporary computer.

REFERENCES

Danner, Peter H. *An Ethics for the Affluent.* Lanham, Md.: University Press of America, 1980.

———. *Getting and Spending: A Primer in Economic Morality.* Kansas City, Mo.: Sheed & Ward, 1984.

Kavanaugh, John F., S.J. *Recovery of Personhood: An Ethics After Post-Modernism.* Milwaukee, Wis.: Center for Ethics Study, Marquette University Press, 1995.

Chapter One

Economic Person before Economics

Economic persons are everyday persons who do economics: they buy and sell; spend and save; borrow and lend; employ and are employed; and so forth. And persons are what we are. For example, Grandpa tried this syllogism on seven-year-old Irene:

Puppy dogs like Christmas chocolates;
But you like chocolates;
Therefore, you are a puppy dog!

"No," Irene pondered, "I am a person!" With that word my sophistry went out the window.

That persons are what we are, and thereby are differentiated from animals, is still obvious to children and was not doubted right up to modern times by most adults, even scholars. Also it was sufficient to see economic persons working and consuming, producing and selling, and gaining and giving to know they were acting economically. On the other hand, it was obvious that their producing, trading, and managing households were also relevant to social and cultural matters and to civic order and peace and were prelude to life beyond the present.

The commentaries of scholars before there were economists, although lacking quantitative and scientific precision, nevertheless present invaluable insights into desirable economic behavior. Implicitly they portray it as both personal and civic but with two specifying notes. Economics is *materialistic* because its object is material, endowed by climate, fertility, geography, and geology. It is *social* because everyone necessarily participates in it as consumer and most will at some time in their lives engage their labor, skills, ideas, and wealth to working material things into goods for use. In this most basic sense these noneconomist scholars contribute an understanding of economic acting as an inherent and necessary element of personal life. This personalist side of economics, therefore, must always be kept in mind as balancing its empirical, quantitative side.

This first chapter will first scan the economic concerns of Old Testament and Christian seers, centering on their insights into the spirit of poverty and its lasting effect on Western culture. Then it will dip into classical philosophic thought, principally Plato and Aristotle, with a passing acknowledgment of the importance of Roman law in defining property rights and commercial concepts. From there it will examine the implications of justice for trading and lending, from the large corpus of Christian philosophic thought, some from Augustine and more from the Medieval and later Scholastics, who in examining these implications adumbrated some basic economic principles. Last, it will survey the thought of a few British and French men-of-affairs, near predecessors of Adam Smith, who began to see economics from a national point of view.

Since contemporary economic science is largely a creation of Western culture, business practice, and scholarship, the discussion of the economic person in this and the following two chapters will generally proceed from that standpoint. Where possible, reference will be made to similar traditions in other cultures, as will be the case in reviewing spiritual poverty.

THE ECONOMICS OF SPIRITUAL POVERTY

The social, political, and economic history of the Israelite nation is inextricably bound to the covenant the Israelites had with their God. This they traced back centuries to Abraham, who was called from Mesopotamia to settle in the present Israeli-Palestinian land. This covenant was reconfirmed with Moses, their great lawgiver and national leader, who led a large number of them out of Egypt after generations of slavery. Initially nomadic intruders into the wilder parts of their new homeland, Israelites after much fighting gradually consolidated their hold over the whole area.

The "Land of Canaan" was probably up to that time in history the most important block of land on earth. It was not only the bridge to three continents but also the link between two of the most ancient foci of civilization, the Tigris-Euphrates and the Nile Valleys. Later it was a keystone in Rome's defensive arc against Persia. As such it lay astride the path of Egyptian and Sudanese merchants and of caravans coming up the Red Sea, heading for Tyre and Sidon and, later, for Antioch and Damascus. While homeland Hebrews without a seaport were engaged in commerce only peripherally, they realized the geopolitical importance for trade of the land God gave them and why Egypt, Babylon, Assyria, Persia, Greece, and Rome fought over their little patch of tough terrain. While glorying in periods of national independence, Israelites were for most of their history under alien sovereignty and dispersed throughout the Western world.

That the Israelites preserved their identity as a people in a land reluctantly fertile and amid the flux of empire, as also did later Jews dispersed throughout the known world, says much for the bonding power of the covenant. As did God's pledge to the whole nation, Israel's faithfulness to it implied family, tribal, and religious convictions of social justice and social charity.

Judeo-Christian Poverty of Spirit

Nothing underscores these tribal bonds and experiences more than the idea and ideal of poverty of spirit. Unlike in contemporary sociology, poverty here is not an economic but an organic concept: accepting one's lot in life while generously relieving others' needs. It is woven of three strands. Penury itself is a scandal, testifying to the wealthy's neglect of their duty to the poor; but general penury may signal God's displeasure at Israel's faithlessness; and finally, true poverty as the mean between riches and penury is the ideal economic state, enough both for one's needs and to help others. Thus, by accepting the covenant and minding justice and charity, the poor in spirit become clients of God, trusting in, open to, and humble before Him. This is the core of an ideal, that has inspired men and women, economic persons both, to lives of justice and generosity to the poor and disadvantaged for nearly three millennia.

The principles of justice the spirit of poverty required are spelled out in the Mosaic moral code, which scholars now confirm reflects earlier Babylonian, Egyptian, and other Middle Eastern codes of laws. But Mosaic law, as reflecting God's covenant, is both more comprehensive and clearer. Moreover, loving and obeying God who, though transcending all powers and principalities, is intimate to their lives demands loving and serving others. These prescriptions are spelled out mainly in Exodus, Deuteronomy, and Ecclesiastes. They very much condition their readers' perspectives about economic persons.

The background for these precepts is a tribal economy in which the overwhelming majority engage in subsistence farming, fishing, and herding. As economic persons they are noted only for the essential crafts but for no export products. Such as it is, their prosperity and increase is owing to God, (Deut. 28:23) who, they should remember, saved them from slavery (Deut. 8:14). Thus they are commanded to be openhanded to the poor and strangers (Deut. 15:11). Leave the harvest fringe to widows, orphans, and strangers (Deut. 24:19–21), and every third year tithe the harvest to support Levites and the poor (Deut. 26:12–13). In dealing with hired workers, pay wages promptly (Deut. 24:15). Do not take as pledge for debt another's livelihood (Deut. 24:10–13). Interest is not to be charged to fellow Israelites and pledged garments are to be returned by sunset (Exod. 22:25–27). Slaves are to be freed in seven years and dismissed with generous help (Deut. 16:12–13). Likewise, debts should be remitted after seven years (Deut. 15:1–2). In sum, Israelites are admonished to respect the poor and to be generous to them. They are warned how difficult it is for merchants, salesmen, and all striving for riches to avoid sin (Sir. 26:29–27:1). Undoubtedly, the Israelites failed these often and grievously. Their generosity, justice, and spirit of poverty needed further testing by adversity.

During the eclipse of Israel, the destruction of the northern kingdom (721 B.C.), the fall of Jerusalem and Babylonian exile (586–538 B.C.), and Judah's client status among the great powers, their spirit of poverty was interiorized. Such disasters forced the Remnant of Israel to realize that the divine promises were not to be fulfilled immediately nor as humanly conceived. This was the lesson taught in Job, the powerful drama of a good man all but destroyed by tragedy, who learns to trust in a God whose ways are beyond human comprehension. The second part of Isaiah goes further in the Songs of the Suffering Servant, telling of one who takes on others' and the community's ills out of love for others and in response to God's call. The Israelites, who heeded these messages, abandoned themselves to God's will, remained hopeful and humble before God, and drew closer together as a community in support of each other. As such it becomes part and parcel of Christian spirituality.

Jesus Christ, whom Christians consider the Suffering Servant incarnate, added the further dimension of *preferring* poverty to wealth. Yet he simply accepted the socioeconomic conditions of his time, the simple living of a village craftsman, and the hand-to-mouth existence of a peripatetic teacher. He numbered among his followers some wealthy people, but his preference was for the poor. Seek, he preached, spiritual rather than material riches, preferring others' well-being to one's own, an example his apostles and disciples emulated. This was especially true of Paul of Tarsus, who asked nothing for his ministry but supported himself by exercising his tent-making craft. But he diligently solicited funds for the impoverished Jerusalem church, urging his Gentile converts to be as generous as their means allowed (2 Cor. 8).

This pragmatic idealism characterized Christianity over the centuries. The asceticism of desert eremites evolved into the monastic life of prayer, work, and charity. "It is a remarkable paradox that such a movement originating as protest against and an escape from culture should become one of the characteristic institutions of Byzantine culture and later of Western Catholicism" (Dawson 1964, 132). Over centuries religious orders pioneered agricultural advances, copied and preserved literature, began the first colleges, engaged the problems of urban poverty, founded hospitals and orphanages, initiated an architectural revolution, and carried the Gospel message across the world. But like the Church itself, religious poverty was never free of abuse and corruption and the need to rejuvenate itself, each rebirth trying to recapture its original ideals by responding to new needs.

Laical, Ecumenical, and Secular

The most universal rebirth was sparked by the Protestant Reformation of the sixteenth century. But reformers like Martin Luther (1483–1546) and John Calvin (1509–64) preached spiritual poverty as a lay ideal for both workers and owners during a time of burgeoning industry and trade. Social reformers like Vincent de Paul (1576–1610), William Wilberforce (1759–1833), Elizabeth Fry (1780–1845), and Don Bosco (1815–88) were each in turn inspired by the spirit of poverty to improve hospital care, to abolish slavery, to reform prisons, and to offer educational opportunity to the poor. Today Mother Teresa symbolizes and inspires in people of means throughout the world a concern to help the poor, whatever their needs and wherever found.

Thus Christians, religious and lay, in the spirit of poverty have regarded the poor as sacramental, seeing Christ in them. Such implies an acceptance of God's will, whatever one's wealth or indigence, but especially cautions the affluent against riches' entanglements. Finally, spiritual poverty is as comprehensive and creative as life itself, seeing even amid affluence new ways of caring for God's poor: drug addicts, alcoholics, AIDS victims, battered and sexually abused spouses, forsaken children, and all those physically and psychically crippled for modern living, besides the penurious in the traditional sense.

Yet poverty of spirit is not an exclusively Judeo-Christian doctrine. Versions appear in all major religions and philosophic systems, ranging from seeing matter as a barrier to ultimate bliss to perceiving it as basic reality. At one extreme Gautama, the Buddha, (563–483 B.C.?) taught the way to nirvana, that is, total absorption into Transcendent Reality, by forsaking all attachments and desires. While only monks can do this, lay people can condition their view of righteousness by observing the moral commandments and by almsgiving, especially to monks, who are by vocation wholly dependent on charity. Change, however, has begun toward "a new sense of social responsibility" by both monks and laity (Küng 1986, 356).

Islamic spirit of poverty is more akin to Judeo-Christianity. Fundamental to Islam is Allah's absolute ownership of everything, which, as servants of Allah, Muslims should strive to increase and multiply. From this they must pay zakat, a tax due to purify the possession of wealth, which is distributed by formula to kin, orphans, the poor, beggars, and wayfarers and to free slaves and support government. Muslims are further "commanded to give charity often and freely" (Denny 1994, 125–6).

At the other extreme is a totally materialistic and secular spirit of poverty. Marx (1818–83), reflecting by rejecting his Jewish heritage and Christian upbringing, cast his basic concept of human sociality in wealth/penury terms: "Poverty is the passive bond which causes the human being to experience the need of the greatest wealth—the other human being" (Marx 1964, 144). On this he grounded his communist principle, "From each according to ability and to each according to need" (Marx 1938, 14). These dogmas are still able to influence economic thought and policy today, even though the people espousing them may be unaware of their source.

Because both religious spiritual poverty and a secularized sense of compassion have had and still have such tremendous, but little-regarded, impact upon contemporary industrialized economies, they justify, despite straying from the chapter's historical format, some comments about the present. But the philanthropy that spiritual poverty and compassion generate are taken for granted or ignored in reviewing the last two centuries, with their most destructive and bloodiest wars in history, their horrible chronicle of class, race, ethnic, and religious persecutions, and their terrible record of crime against children, spouses, neighbors, and fellow citizens which moral viciousness motivates and technology makes possible. Finally, the spectacular growth of industrial economies over the same two hundred years has evoked the greed, envy, and injustice expected of wayward humanity. To repeat: against this awful scene there is a more human picture that is too frequently slighted.

The fact is economic persons in Western states have produced *charity industries* that are unique in human history. However one views charitable giving today, as motivated by a religious spirit of poverty, by a secular sense of compassion, or by a blend of the two, there is no denying its impact on vastly more productive economies than the world has seen before. The largest part of such beneficence consists of transfers of wealth from the well-off to those in need by way of emergency help, educational assistance, retirement aid, medical insurance, family and child support, and the like, which citizens have authorized local, state, and national governments and indirectly international agencies to provide.

Other national and international agencies like the Red Cross, United Way, Oxfam, Salvation Army, Catholic Charities, and others are supported by both private and public contributions. At a more private level are the thousands of foundations, endowed by wealthy families like Ford and Rockefeller, that engage in an array of charitable programs such as scientific research, education, the arts and literature, and public policies. Others, more popular in appeal, invite people to solicit, walk, run, and bike for medical projects, area institutions, and local ventures. Mail appeals for youth and school programs or to support missions, domestic charities, and churches, unknown a half-century ago, proliferate. Natural disasters evoke national and often unsolicited response. Volunteers of all ages and abilities donate untold millions of service hours.

All this philanthropy adds up to a large, though difficult to measure, part of national Gross Domestic Product. Suffice to say, the notion of the stewardship of wealth—that all economic persons are obliged to render some social good by investing surplus wealth or giving it to charity—has taken root in capitalist society. Even more remarkably, despite and more so because of the increase in the world's power to destroy, the meliorist principle is more and more accepted not only by Western nations but worldwide. Increasingly, economic persons are beginning to realize, with shameful exceptions, that ethnic purity, tribalism, xenophobia, conquest, and domination generate more poverty than benefit. The outstanding success of the Cold War's Marshall Plan in jump-starting Germany's and Japan's war-ravaged economies has demonstrated that carrots more often than not are more effective than clubs in producing national and international harmony and in stimulating economic growth.

These comments hardly sanctify all modern free-market mores. But even the most resolute defender of absolute economic freedom and self-interest will not advocate policies of callousness to and unconcern for the poor, such as were practiced in earlier Western economies and still prevail in many survival economies today. How long that compassion could survive a context of adamant, secular libertarianism is open to question, but as of now it still resists any trend toward an *individualism* that totally encapsulates the economic person.

Such a purely secular view of economics in fact mirrors the attitudes of most scholars and philosophers of the Classical Age to economic matters. Not of major interest for any of these scholars and philosophers, economic matters were considered necessary concerns but subsidiary to economic persons' involvement in the city-state's culture and politics. A simple economy (by today's standards) was sufficient for urban living at that time. Yet it serviced the material needs of one of the great advances in Western civilization, the Grecian-Roman city-state, also known in Greek as the *politaea*, which more than any other institution characterized the culture of the Classical Age.

THE ECONOMICS OF THE POLITAEA

Developed in a land fragmented by modest mountain ranges and deep sea indentations, the city-state was a largely self-sufficient economy of people jealously free and proud of their culture and literature. Population pressures on limited space and economic capacity forced a vast colonizing movement all around the Black and Mediterranean Seas. The later conquests by the Macedonian Alexander the Great (356–323 B.C.) planted the Greek ideals of urban living throughout Asia Minor, Syria, Mesopotamia, Persia, Egypt, and Palestine. Rome then carried the city-state idea and ideals to Northern Africa, Spain, Gaul, Britain, and the Rhineland.

The politaea was identified by certain institutions: worship of state gods, political assembly, national festivals and games, education, and cultural opportunities, all materialized in baths, theaters, stadia and gymnasia, political fora, marketplaces, and temples of worship. To these, Roman engineering added sewers, aqueducts, and interconnecting roads. Travel was safe enough to be frequent, and land and sea trade were voluminous.

Some cities of the period were large by any standard—Rome, Alexandria, Antioch, Ephesus—but for most the politaea was of such a size that its political, cultural, and economic elements would be totally blended. The ideal state for Plato (427–347 B.C.) consisted of only five thousand households. Aristotle (384–322 B.C.) held that a state should be of a size that every citizen would know or know of all others. (Foreigners, slaves, and women, of course, were not citizens.) Thus the perspective of the typical economic person was more urban than tribal, more market oriented than agrarian, more outward looking than insular. Plato and Aristotle, therefore, adequately present a conservative and more liberal view of the economics of their day.

Classical Political Economy: Platonic Idealism

Plato, the Athenian aristocrat, as a young man fell under the spell of Socrates (469–399 B.C.), stonemason and self-taught social critic and philosopher. Under him Plato developed his Idealism, the classical philosophy most open to both Judean and Christian moral thought. Piercing the veil of the material world, people must strive to recall a world of Ideal and Eternal Essences, all illuminated by the Idea of the Good. Since people vary in this ability, a natural hierarchy arises in society that reflects the right order in the human soul: passions are subject to appetites, appetites to the will, and the will to the intellect.

Thus, Plato concludes, the state should be governed by the philosopher/kings, those seers who have achieved wisdom. Subject to them are the guardians who police and defend the state. Below them are the masses of citizens who, by obeying the guardians and restraining their own wants, produce a modest well-being for all. The purpose of this hierarchy is to promote people's happiness, which Plato sees first as the cultivation of the moral virtues and only secondly as health, beauty, strength of body, and moderate wealth. In his

Laws, Plato details how a virtuous people and a well-ordered society symbiotically nurture each other.

While he traces the origin of the politaea to the necessity of economic persons to supply basic wants, Plato intends, once moderate well-being is achieved, a zero-growth economy. Land is divided equally and equitably. Trade between producer and consumer can take place only in public markets and at legally fixed prices. To take interest is forbidden, except to penalize debt delinquency. Craftsmen and their customers are enjoined to fulfill contracts. Wealth accumulation is discouraged and excesses may be attached. Retail trade by middlemen, who neither produce nor consume what they sell, while necessary in itself and for reducing commodities to a common measurability in money, leads so easily to injustice and greed that it is forbidden to citizens. Foreigners may engage in it but only within strict regulations (*Laws* XI 1952, 918).

While this last suggests that Plato has some insight into economic value and the function of prices, what emerges clearly from his economic thought is that producing, buying, selling, and consuming, though necessary, are secondary and means to the good life. Christian writers took up and emphasized this subordination of economics to the higher purposes of life. For many it still casts some suspicion on economic exchange, pricing, and values.

Aristotle's Moderate Realism

Aristotle, from an undistinguished family in the provincial seaport of Stagira, was Plato's greatest pupil. But where Plato was poet and visionary, Aristotle was scientific and empirical, lecturing on every known field in his time. While he too based human happiness on moral virtues and contemplating the good, he took people as they are. The happiness all want has many faces: seeking the virtuous mean between vice's too-much and too-little, exercising one's powers of mind and body, and enjoying material goods in moderation. Like Plato, however, his ultimate human happiness consisted in contemplating the Absolute Good.

Regarding persons acting economically, Aristotle was also more in contact with reality than Plato. While agreeing that the state enjoys preeminence over its citizens as whole over parts, he argued against suppressing individuality, because the state is a unity formed from a multiplicity of individuals. Thus he also defended private property against community property and defended trading as necessary for household management and consumption. But since production is for the sake of consumption, producing for exchange is a derived function of commodities, and trading just for profit is unnatural, because these activities lack purpose and transform means into ends. Inevitably the greed to accumulate wealth pampers self-indulgence and often involves gaining unjustly at the expense of others.

Aristotle needed two virtues to govern trade: liberality moderating the use of wealth and justice controlling exchange. As the mean between prodigality and greed, liberality requires gaining wealth justly, using it prudently, and sharing the excess generously (*Ethics* IV 1952, 1–3). Aristotelian justice, in turn, goes beyond an internal rightness to its social implications to guide conduct affecting others. It means, therefore, obeying the laws and customs of society and being fair to others.

This latter requires sharing community goods proportionately to individual merit and trading commodities equal for equal. But since economic persons do not exchange like but unlike goods, commodities must be expressed in common monetary measures, which express the community's estimates of the social value of the producer and of the goods and services publicly offered. Aristotle then argues that freely determined market prices, by expressing community estimates, are just and return both buyer and seller to a condition of well-being equivalent to what they had prior to the exchange. On the other hand, since money's value does not increase when it is lent and repaid, charging interest for a loan is unjust since paying it makes the borrower worse off and the lender better off than before. Like Plato, however, he would charge a penalty for not paying on time.

It is obvious that Aristotle, while more in tune with actual wealth and business activities than Plato, was no less steadfast in examining them from an ethical point of view and assigning a secondary and auxiliary function to economics in creating a just, happy, but basically static society with little consideration for economic growth. While Plato's idealism fit later Christian concern for achieving eternal bliss, Aristotle's moderate realism was a better starting point for resolving the ethical enigmas economic persons meet in this life. Much the same frame of mind provoked renewed interest in that other great classical contribution, the legal framework in which economic activity took place. Like Roman engineering and government it manifests another facet of Roman organizing genius.

Economics and Roman Law

Just as Roman roads and sea routes linked in a physical way the hundreds of city-states, so Roman law united them in a social and political sense. That these diverse peoples functioned as an empire is due largely to the interplay of the *jus civilis,* applying to citizens, with the *jus gentium,* which was an amalgam of the laws and mores of all the peoples under Roman rule. This process accelerated when, in 212, citizenship was granted to all within the

Empire: the two were combined in 395 under Theodosius and then definitively by Trebonianus under Justinian in 533. The *Corpus Juris Civilis*, although it evolved much differently than did English common law, remains, like the Pantheon, as a permanent tribute to Roman genius.

Trials were often more popular and political than judicial. They were heard before politically appointed praetors and argued by special pleaders, more skilled in rhetoric than law. Thorny issues, therefore, were referred to jurisconsults for opinions. Over time they were granted official status, their briefs were codified and quotations from them collated in the *Digestae,* the second part of the *Corpus*. The best legal opinions having been distilled from this huge body of writings, Justinian had all the rest destroyed.

Here, then, were defined the many and complex relations that arise between and among people in their ordinary commercial and civil dealings. It also related the manner of adjudicating them so as to foster peaceful and harmonious living together. Therefore, it tells more about urban economic life and trade in the Empire than the more standard histories of border battles and imperial doings. Besides it contains innumerable and precise analyses of prices, monopoly, interest, usury, loans, contracts, property, trading partnership, and government regulations. All reflect an international economy, that is, one subject to change.

When the *Corpus Juris Civilis* was reintroduced into the West, actually at Bologna in the twelfth century, it almost blew the minds of lawyers wrestling with the mass (often called mess) of vital and living, but generally parochial and often inconsistent, feudal laws and customs. In particular the great canon lawyers of the time such as Gratian, Hostiensis, and Innocent IV used many of the definitions in the *Corpus* in codifying ecclesiastical laws and prescriptions. Since almost all scholars then were clerics, the influence of the *Corpus* was shortly felt not only in civil law but also in moral theology and philosophy and there particularly in discussing exchange justice, just wages, usury, and other such issues.

Thus Classical legal literature, while short on analysis of economic dynamics, yields honed definitions of economic relations. It not only made important contributions to modern commercial law, but became starting points for Medieval ethical debates on exchange, pricing, and lending.

MEDIEVAL ECONOMIC THINKING

As Christianity after Constantine I (306–337) grew to become the dominant but not universal religion in the Roman Empire, the age of the Fathers of the Church was ushered in: Chrysostom, Athanasius, Gregory of Nyssa, and

Basil in the East; Ambrose, Jerome, and Augustine in the West. Augustine's (354–430) personal pilgrimage from classical literature, through Manichaeanism, Neo-Platonism, and finally to his mother's Christianity epitomized the profound transformation the Empire was undergoing: Christianity's triumph and the decline of Roman civilization in the West. In his *Confessions* he plumbs the psychology of a worldly man becoming spiritual and of a good man aspiring to sanctity. His *City of God* argues that a secular society and state bears the seeds of its own demise unless people place their hope and find their joy not just in the politaea but in the eternal city ordained by God.

Economics of the Just Price

Writing in Latin, not Greek, Augustine, more than any other Church Father, was the authoritative voice of Roman Christianity in the Middle Ages. His major effort, demonstrating that concern for this world can be integrated into Christian desires for the next, is critical to the Medieval struggle between ecclesiastical (moral) and civil authority. His few economic *obiter dicta* fit here and become starting points for ethical analysis of exchange. He assumes the right of economic persons to possess private property as caretakers of God's bounty and for sharing with others. He warns against the seductiveness of wealth: used badly, wealth is not possessed but possessing. He is especially hard on profit seeking, suspecting injustice in the search for gain. His remark that the universal vice is to wish to buy cheap and sell dear (Augustine 1963, 314–15) becomes a Medieval standard. Yet he insists that prices, even of slaves, do not reflect commodities' intrinsic natures but people's legitimate needs and even their disordered wants (Augustine 1952, 331a). All told, Augustine holds that the ordinary business of life places no bars to spiritual hopes and "makes this earthly peace bear upon the peace of heaven" (Augustine 1952, 522b).

Augustine died in 430 as Vandals were besieging Hippo, his episcopal see. This was the prelude in Europe to centuries of political chaos, urban decay, illiteracy, shrunken trade, abandoned farmland, and general economic stagnation. Contrasted with Byzantine, Muslim, Chinese, and Indian societies, Europe was barbaric. But parallel to monastic developments, mentioned above, secular society began to come back: invading barbarians were repelled or assimilated; wastelands reconverted; urban life rejuvenated; trade renewed. Since the Church was the sole continuous socializing institution, European civilization was defined by, if not totally faithful to, Christianity. That, as much as a history of struggle, created a sense of solidarity among diverse peoples, even when their lords were warring with each other. This constant struggle to survive also fueled peasants' efforts to protect their rights as well as townspeople's fierce sense of freedom from feudal bonds. For centuries most economic persons struggled in disconnected survival economies, which, however, more and more offered exciting growth possibilities.

Basic to the revival of urban crafts and local and regional trade was the evolution of a broad social principle, specific to economics: free competition among buyers and sellers produced practicable and fair pricing if operating within self-imposed or popularly accepted rules setting business hours, product standards, and working conditions. Here again the emphasis was entirely upon persons as economic agents. Besides a vehement opposition to feudal mandates, the great evil for Medieval burghers was monopolizing, now called unfair competition: *forestalling,* stocking before the market opens; *regrating,* buying ahead of time; and *engrossing,* cornering a market to raise prices. Basic to this truly popular commercial law were concepts of just price, just wages, and usury. These principles were already imbedded in popular convictions as right economic practice when moralists addressed them by way of clarifying their underlying principles.

Ironically, however, moralists, in shoring up this commonsense ethic, made some basic contributions to economic analysis. Thomas Aquinas (1225–74), for example, reasons from the economic person's social nature to the division of economic goods and functions and to the right to private property. Like Aristotle, he argues from the fact of exchange to money as the means of exchange and as a measure of social worth. This arises not from the intrinsic properties of things but from economic persons' needs, from survival more than expedience, from essentiality more than luxury. From exchange's communitarian function, he concludes that either seller or buyer violates justice by taking advantage of the other's need or by the price deviating substantially from community norms. He accepts, nevertheless, that the just price will vary over time and city to city (Aquinas 1920, II–II: q 71). Duns Scotus (1265–1308) rounds this off by insisting that a just price should reward the efforts and risks of bringing goods to market. (Schumpeter 1954, 93).

A century and a half later, Antoninus (1389–1459), though primarily concerned to establish principles for setting or judging a just price, worked out a utility analysis of value, lacking only the concept of marginality. He related value to three factors: a commodity's *effectiveness* for human use; its *scarcity* related to want; and consumers' *anticipated benefit* from it. In addition he saw the price effect of the relative abundance or scarcity of money. His interest in money and money lending was not incidental to his moral philosophy. As Archbishop of Florence, knowing the role the Medici bank played in international commerce, and as creditor to popes and kings, he was prominent in the contemporary debate on the morality of interest and usury (Jarrett 1934, 68–70).

Economics of Interest and Usury

The usury debate, which today seems to be much ado about an obvious business fact and need, wracked the Medieval conscience from as early as Pope Leo I's *Nec hoc quoque* in 435 and probably earlier. A society struggling to survive, whose poor constantly need to borrow from the few rich, soon splits into the many being permanently and progressively in debt to the few. Consequently, the wealthy also amass more wealth by lending instead of working for their money. For Europe in the Dark Ages there was the greater danger of becoming a theocracy, because the Church, monasteries, and especially bishoprics enjoyed continuously mature management.

Thus the usury prohibition was first couched theologically, forbidding charging interest since it violated Christian charity. Charlemagne (742–814) added the secular reason that it is contrary to "the law of the folk." The advent of Aristotle and Roman law revealed new aspects of money lending: being sterile, money cannot create more money; as fungible, all alike, money repaid is identical with money loaned; interest compensates for losses, while usury is a fee for using something that must be returned. Since by lending money, ownership passes to the borrower, lenders would double charge by requiring the return of an equivalent sum of money plus an interest and in that way act unjustly. In this sense both ethical and legal analysis corroborated popular moral convictions that usury was sin against God and man, rather than being bad economics.

But that conclusion more and more conflicted with the growing need for and universality of money borrowing/lending as urban industries developed, wastelands returned to cultivation, and local and international trade expanded. (Much jewelry and many estates were pledged against loans for milord to go crusading.) In response moralists dug deeper into the issue seeking titles to interest. Besides a penalty for late repayments, moral theory very early and generally recognized that actual costs or losses sustained entitled the lender to interest as compensation. While originally most moralists denied title to interest when the possibility of profitable investment is lost by granting a loan, "with the development of commerce and rapidly multiplying opportunities of investment" (Divine 1958, 55), more and more scholars began to accept this right to interest. Risk, the third title to interest, was justified only after risk became generally accepted as inherent in economic enterprise and especially in commercial ventures. Eventually economic persons and scholars saw this as a factor in all lending.

In summary, therefore, the usury debate gradually formulated over centuries of argument the justification of interest-taking in the same terms generally recognized today: the costs the loan entailed, the opportunity costs of lending, and the risks lending and investing involved. The discussion also fixed more firmly in popular convictions that surplus wealth is more benignly and economically used by being invested in financial instruments or as venture capital in new enterprises rather than in lending at interest. Thus, even as the Middle Ages were phasing into the modern and becoming less parochial and personal and more institutional, even nationalistic, in scope, Medieval economic/moral scholars began to adumbrate some of the basic concepts of an abstract economic science (Noonan 1957, 377–8).

ECONOMIC NATIONALISM

Among the many factors contributing to the demise of Medieval Christendom — Renaissance, Reformation, scientific empiricism, an increasingly secular individualism—nationalism is probably the most fundamental. Often identified with royal aegis and ambition, it is more rooted in a people's history, geography, culture, and religion, as Hungarian, Swiss, and Dutch nationalism and most of all that of the American colonies attest. It both spurred and was stimulated by Europe's transglobal discoveries, colonizing, and trade. Together, nationalism and this global perspective added a new and perhaps final dimension to economics and economic persons. Ironically, therefore, economics or better political economy was seen to transcend personal acts and was now written large as management of the nation's economy.

It goes under the name of Mercantilism but it included both state and private spheres. Government officials like Louis XIV's Jean Baptiste Colbert (1619–84) fostered industrial developments and foreign commerce. The private gain seeking of merchants and merchant associations corroborated the goals of government, that selling more to other countries and buying less from them not only increased national wealth (and their own) but abetted royal and national aspirations for territorial aggrandizement, trade monopolies, and colonial empires. This complex of evolving ideas, covered by the term Mercantilism, always had both a state and a private component.

While complementing and collaborating, the two interests were inevitably bound to conflict. National or sovereign goals and needs, especially for manpower and money, soon began to impact on economic persons' expectations of income and wealth. Mercantilism, nonetheless, left the lasting residue that economics is not only a private business and a social concern but also bears particularly on national well-being and international relations. The current domestic and international debates witness the relevance of this economic aspect to life today.

For economic science itself Mercantilism raised questions that generated the first truly scientific economic inquiries: how are national income and wealth measured, how do they circulate, and how are they generated? Sir

William Petty (1623–87), an army physician, was commissioned by Charles II to survey Ireland in order to determine what taxes could be exacted. His curiosity being aroused, upon completing his commission he went on to measure the wealth/productivity of the Irish economy, using as measure a par, or ratio, between land and labor and going on to a complete, if sketchy, picture of the Irish economy: national income growth, tax potentiality, circulation of money, and overall levels of prices, wages, profits, rents, and interests.

Richard Cantillon (1680–1734), a French merchant-financier, knowing Petty, located the economy in a sociopolitical setting, showing how prices, dependent upon the proportion of consumption and production, fluctuate around intrinsic values. The relevant forces determining economic growth are the entrepreneurial spirit of the free farmers set against the general lifestyle, largely set by that of the great landowners: the more lavish this lifestyle, the slower economic growth; the more frugal, the faster. What in Petty and Cantillon was disjointed, Francois Quesnay (1694–1774) organized into a numerical model, his famous *Tableau Economique*. Rightly, it is honored as the first circular flow macroeconomic model. With it economic science may be said to have begun.

Still very primitive, Quesnay's model represents the economy as a system into which mainly free farmer/entrepreneurs feed raw materials and labor. The net product yielded is then distributed throughout the economy: rent to landlords, wages to farm labor, income to merchants and manufacturers, and wages to their labor. Countering the flow of product, the money that all the economic orders spend works its way back to the farmers, starting a new cycle of investment, production, and distribution. For all its heroic assumptions and abstractions, Quesnay's model provided an organon for identifying and addressing questions about production, exchange, consumption, money, and the rest, abstracted from their being embedded in the total life of the community. Smith thought it so important that he intended to dedicate the *Wealth of Nations* to Quesnay, had the good doctor not died before publication.

The view from the *Tableau,* looking back over more than two millennia, may not be breathtaking but neither is it bleak and dreary. For sure it presents many pleasing vistas of how economics fits into all phases of the lives of economic persons. Managing the material side of life is essential for both personal and family goals, and sharing one's goods is a way of respecting others as fellow human persons. Economic wealth moderately used is essential for both civil order and virtue. Justice and liberality in producing and exchanging goods and services and in lending money are both the subjects of many, if not most, of the legal and political ties, which not only are basic to business relations and organizations but bind people socially.

Looking forward, the *Tableau* presents the unending task of analyzing all its operational elements: enterprise, investment, production techniques, labor relations, and changing consumer needs and wants, with money as the operational fuel. In addition, the model demands continuous empirical research to update the ever-changing numbers and ratios for these economic categories. In short, the economic model calls for an economic science, which, though demanding and fascinating in its own terms, nevertheless must service all the human and personal needs which economic persons engaged in long before there were economists to analyze their activities.

REFERENCES

Aquinas, Thomas. *Summa Theologica* (II–II, Q 66–77). Translated by the Fathers of the English Dominican Province. New York: Benziger, 1920.

Aristotle. *Nicomachean Ethics.* Translated by W. D. Ross. Great Books of the Western World, ed. Robert Maynard Hutchins. Chicago: Encyclopedia Britannica, 1952.

——. *Politics.* Translated by B. Jowett. Great Books of the Western World, ed. Robert Maynard Hutchins. Chicago: Encyclopedia Britannica, 1952.

Augustine. *The City of God.* Translated by M. Dodds. Great Books of the Western World, ed. Robert Maynard Hutchins. Chicago: Encyclopedia Britannica, 1952.

——. *De Trinitate.* Translated by S. McKenna. Washington, D.C.: Catholic University of America Press, 1963.

Barr, Stringfellow. *The Will of Zeus.* Philadelphia: J. B. Lippincott Co., 1961.

Burns, G. Delisle. *The First Europe: A Study of the Establishment of Modern Christendom.* London: Allen & Unwin, 1947.

Calvin, John. *Institutes of the Christian Religion.* Edited by J. T. McNeill and translated by F. L. Battles. Library of Christian Classics, vol. 20. Philadelphia: Westminster, 1960.

Dawson, Christopher. *The Formation of Christendom.* New York: Sheed & Ward, 1964.

Dempsey, Bernard W., S.J. *The Functional Economy: Bases of Economical Organization.* Englewood Cliffs, N.J.: Prentice Hall, 1958.

Denny, F. M. *An Introduction to Islam.* 2d ed. New York: Macmillan, 1994.

Divine, Thomas F., S.J. *Interest: An Historical & Analytical Study in Economics & Modern Ethics.* Milwaukee,Wis.: Marquette University Press, 1958.

Gelin, Albert. *Les Pauvres de Yahve.* Paris: Les Editions du Cerf, 1955.

Grelot, Pierre. "La Pauvrete dans L'Ecriture Sainte." *Christus* 8, n.d.

Heckscher, Eli F. *Mercantilism.* Translated by M. Shapiro. London: Allen & Unwin, Ltd., 1935.

Humbert, Alphonse, CSSR. "L'attitude des premiers chretiens devant les biens temporels." *Studia Moralia* 4, n.d.

Jarrett, Dom Bede. *S. Antonino and Medieval Economics.* London: Mauresa, 1934.

The Jerusalem Bible. Garden City, N.Y.: Doubleday, 1966. All references are to this edition.

Küng, Hans, Josef van Ess, Heinriech von Stietencron, and Heinz Bechent. *Christianity and the World Religions: Paths to Dialogue with Islam, Hinduism, and Buddhism.* Translated by P. Heinegg. New York: Doubleday, 1986.

Marx, Karl. *A Critique of the Gotha Programme.* Edited by C. P. Dutton. New York: International Publishers, 1938.

———. *Economic and Philosophic Manuscripts of 1844.* Edited by D. Struick and translated by M. Milligan. New York: International Publishers, 1964.

Monroe, Arthur E., ed. *Early Economic Thought: Selections from Economic Literature prior to Adam Smith.* Cambridge, Mass.: Harvard University Press, 1930.

Mulhern, Philip, O. P. *Dedicated Poverty: Its History and Theology.* New York: Alba House, 1970.

Noonan, John T. Jr. *The Scholastic Analysis of Usury.* Cambridge, Mass.: Harvard University Press, 1957.

Peters, F. E. *The Harvest of Hellenism: A History of the Near East from Alexander the Great to the Triumph of Christianity.* New York: Simon & Schuster, 1970.

Pirenne, Henri. *Medieval Cities.* Garden City, N.Y.: Doubleday, 1956.

Plato. "The Republic and Laws." In *The Dialogues of Plato.* Translated by B. Jowett. Great Books of the Western World, ed. Robert Maynard Hutchins. Chicago: Encyclopedia Britannica, 1952.

Rand, E. K. *Founders of the Middle Ages.* Cambridge, Mass.: Harvard University Press, 1928.

Schumpeter, Joseph A. *History of Economic Analysis.* Edited from manuscript by E. B. Schumpeter. New York: Oxford University Press, 1954.

Yonick, Stephen, O.F.M. *Introduction to Covenant with God's Poor.* Translated by Auspicius van Corstanji and G. Reidy, O.F.M. Chicago: Franciscan Herald Press, 1966.

Chapter Two

Economic Science, Economic Person

This chapter celebrates economics' rite of passage from being just a topic, albeit extensive, in religious, philosophical, political, or nationalist studies to a fully fledged empirical and mathematical social science. That, in turn, has the consequence that the economic person tended to disappear into the abstractions of *homo economicus.*

The start of this process can be located, as well as anywhere, in the thought and writing of the Scots moral philosopher Adam Smith (1723–90). His most important work, *An Inquiry into the Nature and Causes of the Wealth of Nations,* appeared the year the first of many European colonies declared its independence. His initial success over other contenders like Steuart's *An Inquiry into Principles of Political Economy* (1767) or Lauderdale's *An Inquiry into the Nature and Origin of Public Wealth* (1804) was sustained over a generation of revolution and war on the Continent. It is still a must for any economic scholar.

The metastasis in economic thought that it began, for sure, found a favorable climate in the Industrial Revolution that was already under way in England by 1800 and was shortly to take root in the United States and on the Continent. Besides the impact of industrialism, economic thinking began to reflect sciential and secularist currents, the other important element of the nineteenth-century Zeitgeist. Thus starting with Smith, economic science began to take the form that is now standard in most study programs and in most elementary text books.

ADAM SMITH AND AFTER

Adam Smith is indeed an appropriate starting point. As moral philosopher, he condemned casuistic intellectualism, the attempt to fashion ethics by the case method. Instead he preferred to follow natural sentiments and feelings as pragmatic moral guides. As a political economist, he rejected the rigid rationalism of the *economistes* while honoring Quesnay's *Tableau Economique*. Rather, his genius was to flesh out the abstract macroeconomic models of Petty, of Cantillon, and especially of Quesnay with real-life actions, hopes, and relations. For Smith the economy is a wealth-creating system, integral to persons' private and public lives by providing for their material needs and wants. Thus he framed the context for subsequent economic discussion and set the tone of economic analysis. Indeed, his most frequently cited conceptions have become part of economic folklore. Even today the *Wealth of Nations* can yield a sense that economics is a truly social science.

His "obvious and simple system of natural liberty" (Smith 1937, 651) most clearly identifies his economics as a behavioral science. For Smith the concept of sympathy or fellow feeling, that people can surmise others' good by discerning their own is the principle underlying all personal and social relationships (Smith 1853, 3). It implies that persons are best able to judge what serves their own interest (Smith 1853, 312) and consequently can be concerned about and happy for others' good fortune, although benefiting from neither (Smith 1853, 3). Both principles fit well his easy system of nature in that the economic person, being endowed with an affinity for socially beneficial goals, has been given an "appetite for the means by which alone the end can be brought about" (110). Together benevolence and a virtuous self-interest "necessarily pursue the most effectual means for promoting the happiness of mankind" (264).

Smith then invests economic behavior generally with social harmony. Indeed, his much castigated Invisible Hand is really an expression of it. While seemingly tolerating selfishness, Smith stresses the social benefit which inheres in all economic actions. A person, in producing things of great value although only intending personal gain, "frequently promotes that of Society more effectually than when he really intends to promote it" (Smith 1937, 423). From the interworking of sympathy and self-interest, he concludes that "every man . . . is fitter and abler to take care of himself than any other person" (Smith 1853, 321). This applies particularly to "the desire of bettering our condition, which . . . comes with us from the womb, and never leaves us until we go into the grave" (Smith 1937, 324).

Such self-interest, however, is served not by addressing the "humanity of the butcher, brewer, and baker, but their self-love and . . . advantage" (14). Indeed the rich "consume little more than the poor and in spite of their material selfishness and rapacity . . . make nearly the same distribution as would have been done with equal distribution" (Smith 1853, 264). Thus a system of gain seeking, due to rather than despite self-interest, will yield a prospering economy, so that the workers who feed, clothe, and house others are "themselves tolerably well fed, clothed, and lodged" (Smith 1837, 79). Smith's self-interest is other relating.

All in all, therefore, while Smith is well aware of a selfish bias in human nature, he tends to see more light than shadows. Despite economic persons' striving for fortunes, even at cost to others, as paths to the good life, Smith sees the economy as so balancing between seeking and sought, between providing and consuming, that it can be left to itself. As a self-perpetuating system fueled by basic personal instincts and feelings, outside controls, whether moral or social, are for the most part unnecessary. For Smith, economic science was simply analysis of *economic praxis*.

This Smithian optimism prevailed into the eighteenth century and is still honored, although much of his economic paraphernalia such as labor theory of value, division of labor, laissez-faire, economic harmony, and frugality gradually became shopworn and were discarded. What remained after this patina was worn away in the furnaces and sweatshops of the Industrial Revolution was an empirical science of a self-determining process, propelled by production and incomes and governed by laws impervious of moral principles. How so and what hence is the story still to be told.

Post-Smithian Economics

David Ricardo (1772–1823), the most capable of many Smithian commentators, did adhere to his free market ideology. A retired stockbroker, however, thinking by and following numbers, he punctured Smith's optimism with the simple mathematical analysis that, with fixed limits to land, economic growth would inevitably slow to stagnation. Another early Smithian, the Genevan historian Jean Charles Sismondi (1773–1842), in his *Nouveaux Principes d'Economie Politique* (1819), seeing how the lot of workers was ravaged by mechanization and periodic recessions, argued for moderate state welfarism. Thus Smith's laissez-faire economy was shown in theory and in fact prone to reward personal effort inequitably and inevitably to produce depressions.

Later theorists from both ends of the ideological spectrum went further in disjoining personal purposes from scientifically assumed behavioral premises. Whatever peoples' personal motives, they were subsumed under broad function categories. Thus Nassau Senior (1790–1864), in his *Outline of the Science of Political Economy* (1836), though much involved in advising government on poverty, education, health, and housing policies, derives his economic analysis from four abstract human tendencies: people will maximize wealth at least cost; people, especially the poor, will procreate up to subsistence limits; the saving/investing tendency of the wealthy tend to yield increasing returns; while land and labor of the masses yield diminishing returns. Altogether these tendencies will have the inevitable effect that the rich will get richer and the poor poorer.

Nothing underscored this conviction more surely than the decision by Charles Trevelyan, the Permanent Secretary to the Treasury, to deny further relief to the Irish dying daily by the thousands during the Potato Famine of 1845–47 because such relief would distort the working of free trade (Nankivell 1995, 102). By that time Smith's unfettered personalist economy had become a scientific autarchy.

Already, economists had driven a wedge between economic theory and public welfare, and theorists on the right had taken that for gospel. Then Karl Marx (1818–83) took it to its inevitable conclusion. He developed from the Hegelianism of his youth a dialectical materialism of the interaction of labor, as the creative force, with capital as the demiurgic exploiter of surplus value. Since the dialectic tends to periodic overproduction, generating more capital concentration and wider proletarian misery, the dialectic presses on until the last exploiter is exploited and communism, the classless society of plenty, dawns. Thus, while Marx deplored proletarian poverty and castigated capitalistic greed, in his analysis Smithian human tendencies, desires, and action have transformed into and function as impersonal and cosmic forces in a materialistic dialectic, producing universal prosperity. It is as if the economic person has disappeared.

John Stuart Mill (1806–73), while nourished on Smith and espousing economic freedom, was no less scientifically utopian than Marx. The epitome of the "Victorian Compromise," his idea of society embraced all the major eighteenth-century currents: Utilitarianism, Positivism, Socialism, Economic Liberalism, and Romanticism. Like Senior, Mill conceived "economic man" (*homo economicus*) as naturally free and governed by abstract tendencies in generating and using wealth. Like Marx, he saw humanity (not necessarily all persons) progressing toward a golden age of shared but stable abundance, harmonized with nature and guided by benevolent government. All told, it conjures up Smithian optimism but in an abstract, utopian setting of scientific speculation.

Rejecting much of this, marginal utility economists of the 1870s sought to uncover the common core of all economic acts. They held that economic value is a function of the amount of a good already had and the expected benefit from more of it: its marginal utility. But Friedrich von Wieser (1851–1926) attempted to do this by abstracting from all incidental elements and considering utility only (Wieser 1927, 3–9). Leon Walras (1834–1910) implicitly did the same by casting all of utility value theory into a system of simultaneous equations, which by a series of competitive price changes produces general equilibrium in all resource and product markets. This model of the economy as an integrated quantitative system Schumpeter called a work comparable "with the achievements of theoretical physics" (Schumpeter 1954, 827). However that may be, with Smith's behavioral model being cast in a quantitative mold, *economics as an empirical science* had come into being.

Given that, it is appropriate, having started with Smith, to highlight another Olympian, Alfred Marshall (1842–1924). In linking Smith, Ricardo, and Mill to the marginal utility school and pointing to future theoretical and empirical developments, he towered over a generation of economists. For sure, his basic concern as an economist was ethical and humanitarian and as a mathematician he knew numbers' limitations as measures of desire and satisfaction. Yet he insisted that only statistically observable facts be used in economic analysis. Also, with his partial equilibrium system and its box of analytical tools, he fashioned powerful instruments to further both empirical and theoretical analysis and to assist formulating economic policy. Despite his ethical leanings, Marshall created a mathematical and empirical organon driven by universal economic principles. For many Marshall is the economist.

But unpredictably, many of his Cantabrigian students like Pigou, Hawtrey, Robertson, and the Robinsons, shocked by World War I and the Great Depression, turned back to the study of political economy—that is, viewing the economy as a system of interacting public tendencies. They thus opened the way for government intervention in the economy. Contributing most to this effort was John M. Keynes (1883–1946) whose kit of analytic creations such as propensity to consume, aggregate effective demand, liquidity preference, marginal efficiency of capital, equilibrium level of employment, and similar abstract tendencies proved of supreme worth in explaining the inner workings of and interrelationships among trillionnaire national economies.

But in the process individual ambition and effort, personal goals, and purposes are subsumed into the whole with the seeming result that the economy can be directed from above and that businesses, families, and persons can be macromanaged by government bureaucrats. Thus, Adam Smith's optimistic and behavioristic political economy, in which government's role is nugatory, has really given place to an anxious psychometric macroeconomy, where public spending, taxing, and monetary policy are decisive.

This recounting of economics' conversion from a disjointed subject to a complex but integrated science could have included the contributions of hundreds of other scholars and interpreted those listed here differently. It is simply intended to show how economic theorizing drifted from a personalist to an abstract quantitative study. Marshall's *Principles of Economics* and Keynes's *General Theory*, contrasted to the *Wealth of Nations*, demonstrate clearly how dramatically the presentation of economic science has changed over more than a century. While no economist suggests that personal motives and moral purposes can be ignored, it is also true that since Smith, the quantitative and empirical side of economics has come to the fore while the introspective and personalist has receded. The *economic person* became *homo economicus*.

The elegant processes of microeconomics with its utilities, costs, schedules, elasticities, equilibria, incomes, and profits seem to behave independently of the real world of unemployment and work, failure and success, greed and charity. In the temples of national income analysis the high priests of monetary and macrotheory scrutinize the economy's quantitative entrails to prognosticate its future course, as the more effective analysis of the short run than sampling peoples' moods and intentions. In this respect too, economists are completely in tune with popular understanding of what economics is all about.

Economists, when asked how the economy is doing, are not expected to explain how the economy, as a complex network of people buying and selling, working and managing, and saving and investing, use labor and resources to produce the goods and services others want. But their opinions are sought about what employment, sales, and profit trends say; what leading indicators portend; and whatever other schedules, correlations, functions, or ratios they might find useful to explain and predict what course the economy is taking. In short, economists while agreeing their science deals with the activity and conduct of economic persons, will insist that *homo economicus* abstracts from most personal motivations except the rationality of marginality and gain seeking and is thus restricted to acts expressible in numbers.

In this they are right on point. Economics is a mathematical science; it deals with material things and with actions taking place over time, all of which must be weighed, measured, counted, and timed. Thus polls, trends, and models give a better picture of what the economy is doing than accounts of personal successes and failures and theories of what motivates acts. Economists as economic scientists, however, are a very small group contrasted to economic practitioners who include everyone. In other words, just as one must distinguish between what health-care scientists and providers recommend and what ordinary people, the health-care practitioners, do or fail to do to maintain good health, so one must distinguish between economists' analysis of the internal working of the economy and the decisions and actions of economic persons who consume, work, and invest. In other words, economics must be seen as both science and praxis.

In this respect, moreover, economists, like other scientists, are being influenced by and in tune with the Zeitgeist, the sociological and intellectual climate of the last two centuries. While it is essential for economics' transit from just a body of learning to being a true science, the age's Zeitgeist also incorporated economic science as an integral element.

THE PREVAILING ZEITGEIST

No one doubts that today's Western civilization differs from the great Hindu, Muslim, and Chinese civilizations and from those of its own Medieval and Classical periods. Scholars do disagree over the complete listing of distinguishing features and the factors initiating change from one culture to the next. Similarly the Zeitgeist, the intellectual and moral climate, differs from one age to another and there is little agreement about all their differences or their relative weight and import. Nevertheless, there are usually a few salient features, to which all can agree and which are sufficient in themselves to distinguish a period's culture from those of prior or later times. For the purpose here, three words adequately characterize the Zeitgeist when economics reached scientific maturity. They are *scientism*, *industrialism*, and *secularism*. They should be understood here not as discrete intellectual tendencies but as mutually qualifying and blending into each other.

The scientific revolution is industrialized and together they revolutionize secular living. Scientism, as a restless drive, probes ever further into how humans act and the universe runs. Technologists then translate this accumulating knowledge into practical uses to cure diseases and extend life, to improve communication and travel, to increase agricultural productivity, to shape the terrain, and to build ever faster, safer, and higher. Industrialism, the practical application of scientific knowledge, inevitably and irreversibly revolutionizes what and how goods and services are produced and the power of nations to dominate.

Industry as war power was early revealed in the Civil War, when the more industrialized North overwhelmed the more agricultural South. For the first time in history, also, more pacific but industrialized nations are really protected against more aggressive but less civilized predators. The industrialized need only fear each other! Except for that, science and industry together have made living more pleasurable and less at the mercy of natural forces.

It is easy to glamorize the simpler life of just two hundred years ago as more attuned to nature. But the realities of malls contrasted to village markets, modern housing—even the poorest—to peasant cottages and laborers' hovels, today's travel to walking and carting, and contemporary health care to reliance on primitive doctoring and popular herbs and nostrums all favor contemporary economies' greater knowledge, larger scale, and more complex production. Each such improvement, in turn, requires better management of labor, closer work collaboration, and more refined employment. Above all, these revolutions in production and trade, first nationally and then internationally required better methods of financing worldwide commerce and better means of paying than by bullion, which is costly to safeguard and transfer, or by government money, which is subject to political needs and whims.

Indeed this financial revolution fulfills a dream older than that of walking on the moon but actually realized, though imperfectly, before that great event. It grew from the hope and effort to develop ways of safeguarding wealth and even increasing it by lending it safely. Possible between family members or friends, most such credit/debt transactions require an intermediary, who can guarantee the loan and has means to coerce repayment. Given the need for *trust and trustworthiness*, economic persons first turned to religious institutions, like Apollo's temple at Delphi, and later to monasteries and religious orders. As the needs of sovereigns increased and maritime and long-distance trade grew, more secular companies like the Fuggers and Medici began to dominate. Thus, despite a history of mismanagement and gross chicanery, banking has proliferated over the globe and *bank credit/debt* has become a universal means of exchange; its use value is its exchange value.

Lest the point be lost: the global changes industrialism has produced become possible only as economic and business *trust* has increased. This habit may well be solidified for moral reasons but it can prevail based only on the secular consideration that borrowing/lending is possible and can become commonplace only by universally guaranteeing repayment. Nothing in this world can be made perfect and is even less so when human motivation is involved. But the credit/debt system has worked well enough to finance the period of greatest industrial growth in human history. Such is an economic sea change of the first order.

Naturally, therefore, economics plays a larger part in life. Economic persons are more eager to possess the goods of this life, more anxious about their material welfare (often to the disregard of others) and thus more concerned about this life and less about any hereafter. For many people, if not most, religious beliefs are more *pro forma* than real. Concern for others and care of the environment—both still integral to religious convictions—are for the majority, while sincerely held, only secular matters. For many people, too, such morality in principle, practice, and purpose is just a this-world business. While peoples and nations have experienced periodic bursts of religious fervor, even then their material, social, and political problems tended to be seen as concerns of this mortal life only, with little eternal implication.

The spread of such thinking, together with strict separation of state and church in most Western nations, means that religion is more and more confined to private life. It is axiomatic for many individuals, if not most, that religious convictions are not relevant to and should not, therefore, intrude upon economic, political, and academic questions. If religion plays any role in modern living, it is to ease people over life's rough spots: economic hardships, strained social relations, serious pathology, and inevitable death. Religion may speak about an afterlife, but that is scientifically unproven and little relevant to the reality of industrial living.

In sum, scientism, industrialism, and secularism in enhancing the material side of life have tended to contract the spiritual. Since the spiritual and moral pertain to life's ultimate purpose, the responsibility of persons as agents who fashion their moral, social, political, and, of concern here, their economic life, has also been diminished. And since the Zeitgeist also permeates the other social sciences, such as physiology, psychology, and sociology, they in turn tend to color economic practice and theory.

The desire of social scientist to emulate the observation, measurement, and analytical methods of the physical sciences has, of course, generated a vast store of useful knowledge about human beings and their cultures, habits, and relations. This preference for empirical over introspective analysis avoids some of the more benighted conclusions of Classic and Medieval science and detours around the swamp of the materialism/idealism controversy.

EMPIRICISM AND THE SOCIAL SCIENCES

In this respect all the social sciences are largely owing to Auguste Comte (1798–1857) for pioneering an empirical philosophy. Bypassing Descartes's problem, he avoided endless controversy by limiting "true" knowledge to the positive sciences. His positivism stressed three points: empiricism, the experience of facts, is the only real knowledge; mechanical or impersonal causes are preferred explanations; and using logic and mathematics eliminates subjective bias (Evans 1977, 16–7). By applying these to his science of sociology he aimed to emulate the achievements of the natural sciences. His ideas in turn spurred the growth of a galaxy of other studies—biology, physiology, psychology, and their subsciences, all of which have accumulated vast stores of knowledge about how humans relate to their environment and to each other.

More to the point, this positivistic approach to the study of people tends to have the same effect on economics: to a more materialistic and less moral perception of economic persons. While considerations from biology and the other social sciences touch economic science only peripherally, they do influence it contextually. Economists cannot but know of the vast new knowledge empirical methods have generated in physiology, psychology, and sociology and thus to be enticed into exploring their implications for economic science. The positivistic fervor in the social sciences generally has abetted economics' empirical and quantitative tilt.

The awesome new knowledge of human biology and physiology, like mapping the brain and nervous system, DNA, reproductive and hormonal research, and the other spectacular advances in medicine now, is able to assign physical causes for conditions and symptoms which two centuries ago were ascribed to mental and spiritual causes. Such discoveries obviously have changed the understanding of how economic persons work, play, and consume. Schumpeter lists four areas where biological research has modified economic speculation (Schumpeter 1954, 788–92).

First, he cites the preferability of the biological concept of 'organism' as stressing the economy's vital nature over any kind of mechanistic analogy. Yet, the economy as organism tends to reduce economic persons' individualities in favor of their functioning as a group. Even more so, biometrical research in areas of *eugenics and ethnicity*, while spurring studies on the issue of nature versus nurture and on questions of whether and, if so, how racial characteristics affect varying rates of economic progress, further stresses cultural, environmental, and tribal factors over personal and individual abilities and motivation.

Finally, the development in nineteenth-century biology of most consequence for economic sociology was the advent of Darwinism. The assertion that in capitalism the economic fittest to survive are the most competitive is more valid compared to the egalitarianism of state socialism. But it begs the question of whether such fitness to survive makes for more social desirability. In sum, while the spectacular biological developments over the last two hundred years have had more circumstantial than fundamental influence on economic theory, they still tended to highlight the roles of the generalized class or group and to lessen those of individual economic persons.

More relevant to the concept of the economic person is the phenomenal growth of empirical psychology, which Sigmund Freud's pioneering studies accelerated. Freud (1856–1939) sees consciousness as a small and derivative part of mind, which is largely unconscious and ultimately derived from one's primary instincts of self-preservation, sex, gregariousness, and hunger. In insisting that the nature of humans can ultimately be grasped only by empirical investigation, Freud parts from a personalist view of the individual in a fundamental way: the physical predominates at the expense of the spiritual (Evans 1977, 42–3). The Freudian system and psychoanalysis, nevertheless, did point out new directions in psychological research.

Behaviorism is the culmination of the process of substituting empirical observation, measurement, and scientific laws for the introspective methods which were dominant in psychology in the nineteenth century (Evans 1977,

47). B. F. Skinner's (1904–90) stimulus/response mechanism explains behavior in terms of the individual's physiological makeup and his or her responses to or effects on the environment. Skinner, in sweeping away Freud's ego, superego, and id, concludes that a human being is just a biological organism, conditioned by the environment to respond to it in a variety of ways (Evans 1977, 52–3). Consequently, since economic persons are viewed as possessing neither effective consciousness nor free will, their economic actions are inevitably and only subject to mathematical formulation and analysis. The economic person has become *homo economicus*.

The sociology of Emile Durkheim (1858–1917), following Comte, went even farther. In defining social relations in the same sense as physical objects, Durkheim holds that social facts by way of social controls, social functions, ideology, and culture mold human conduct more than personal intentions and natural needs. Thus a person's beliefs, values, and moral principles are relative to the culture and group to which one belongs and one's actions are determined by the cultural role one plays (Evans 1977, 61–6). As applied to economic action, Durkheim's cultural determinism, like Skinner's behavioralism, makes *homo economicus*, as self-interested seeker of economic gain, react only to changing economic conditions.

All the preceding point the same way. Since empirical research and the technology it spawned have improved human livelihood beyond imagining two centuries ago, science has for many people replaced moral convictions and religious faith as the source of certitude. Scientists are able to counteract some of nature's most destructive forces and to put others to human use. Empirical methods have revolutionized work, travel, communication, nourishment, and life expectancy: in short, what people know and expect from life. More of consequence psychologically for *homo economicus* is that the constant anticipation of having more and of living better means that any decrease in the rate of economic growth or, worse, a decline, becomes a cause for national alarm.

But if empirical methods have produced what some might call the best of times in human history, they have contributed also to the worst of times. The rate of infant mortality has been dramatically decreased but millions of private and state-ordered abortions are performed annually. Medical wonders have almost doubled life expectancy; at the same time abusive health habits are cutting lives short. Homes are more comfortable, while family living has deteriorated. The store of human knowledge has vastly increased but much education is shoddy and people are ruled more and more by advertising, ballyhoo, and propaganda.

No similar period in human history has experienced the amount of public and private tyranny, killing, and destruction. Never before has such a large part of the human race been subjected to totalitarian despotism. Two centuries of almost constant warfare, revolutions, and rebellions included four of the most lethal and destructive wars in history. To this must be added a string of tribal, ethnic, and religious purges and a sad record of private killings, assassinations, terrorism, gang fights, traffic deaths, and domestic violence. The effect of this public and private mayhem has been to force millions of people to risk unimaginable suffering in fleeing their homelands. By contrast Viking raids, Gothic conquests, and Turkish onslaughts now seem minor events.

This toll of death and destruction owes much to modern science and its devastating technologies. But the mind-set empiricism fosters perhaps bears greater responsibility. While empirical research in economics and the other social sciences has increased people's understanding of their potentialities and makeup, laid bare the psyche's depth and complexity, and showed the impact of culture, environment, gender, and race on how people think and act, this flood of exciting empirical knowledge of humans' physical natures tends to block introspective understanding of how moral and spiritual faculties are guides for living. Conversely, the know-how which gives power causes many of today's movers and shakers to ignore virtues generally as well as considerations of others' humanity.

ECONOMIC SCIENCE AND PRAXIS

All of this, as one would expect, is reflected in today's economic science. While all economic acts terminate in transactions which must be measured quantitatively, nevertheless, the economic person is an agent with all the good and bad of ideas, ambitions, wants, and relations that go with being a person. To count and judge economic acts only mathematically, therefore, is to ignore their moral content or, at best, to resort to amoral relativism based on averages. Since the average as moral norm is in constant flux, it presents a behavioral impasse for anyone concerned about the morality of conduct as expressed in a code of ethics.

In other words, ethics and economics, despite popular skepticism, are paired: ethics the science of moral choice; economics that of utilitarian choice. Ethics fashions rules for behaving in life's changing phases, for being just and kind to others, and for clarifying and achieving life-goals. Economics, on the other hand, guides by using abilities gainfully, by reaching desired levels of living, and by acquiring adequate amounts of wealth. Together they constitute for most people the precepts that control their lives' principal agenda. Other goals and purposes can add status, grace, and dignity to life, but ethics and economics are foundational.

Obviously they interact, ideally collaborating but often at variance. But no economic person can be fully integrated where these precepts regularly work at cross purposes. Since economic persons make both ethical and economic choices, the rules of both economics and of ethics focus on and are derived from the nature of human persons. To understand how they relate, therefore, needs answers to such questions as what are persons, what is their ultimate good and purpose for being, and what psychic and social means are available to achieve them.

Neither view, of course, is complete or adequate by itself. A purely personalist approach ignores the hard fact that economic acts must be timed and expressed in mathematical rations: so much of one thing exchanged for or related to so much of another. On the other hand, since the economy consists of economic persons managing households, businesses, and governments, economic acts are social, personal, and purposive. However the numbers suggest the appropriate course of action, the economy is still drama: prospering ambition or bitter failure, resolute or timid enterprise, easy or hostile cooperation, arrogant or humane management, prodigal or reasonable consumption.

Conversely, it cannot be overemphasized that economics is a quantitative science. Because economic acts always involve the exchange or trade-off of what is physically measured—work, resource, commodities, and risks—every act produces a ratio: so much for so much. A person, therefore, acts economically *ratio*-nally by choosing the more desired combination of what is gained for what is surrendered. Recalling again how Western economies have changed over two centuries or so from a patchwork of local and regional markets in the frailest national frameworks to the huge national and global economies today will underscore the importance and absolute necessity of the sophisticated modeling, correlating, and trending of the daily deluge of quantitative and empirical facts economists savor. Without their daily processing, modern economies would be in chaos. Rightfully, honors, grants, and prizes have gone mainly to mathematically oriented economists.

While the analytic waves over the last two hundred years or so rolled toward the quantitative and empirical, however, still an undertow continued to express concern for and interest in economics' other polarity, its humanistic and personalist side. Indeed, since the Great Depression economics has experienced a growing groundswell of research into the social, cultural, and moral implications of economic thought. Just a survey of the intellectual landscape and review of economists, who kept this humanistic tradition alive, will help correct the conception of economics as only a quantitative science and also serve as bridge to viewing the subject from a personalist perspective.

REFERENCES

Evans, C. Stephen. *Preserving the Person: A Look at the Human Sciences*. Downers Grove, Ill.: InterVarsity Press, 1977.

Marshall, Alfred. *Principles of Economics*. New York: Macmillan, 1890.

Marx, Karl. *Capital*. Translated by S. Moore and E. Aveling, and edited by Friedrich Engels. Great Books of the Western World, ed. Robert Maynard Hutchins. Chicago: Encyclopedia Britannica, 1952.

Mill, John Stuart. *Principles of Political Economy*. Boston: Little, Brown, 1848.

Nankivell, Owen. *Economics, Society, and Values*. Aldershot, England: Avebury, 1995

Ricardo, David. *The Principles of Political Economy and Taxation*. Homewood, Ill.: Richard D. Irwin, 1963.

Roll, Eric. *A History of Economic Thought*. 3d ed. London: Faber, 1953.

Schumpeter, Joseph A. *History of Economic Analysis*. Edited from manuscript by E. B. Schumpeter. New York: Oxford University Press, 1954.

Smith, Adam. *The Theory of Moral Sentiments*. London: Henry G. Bohn, 1853.

———. *An Inquiry into the Nature and Causes of the Wealth of Nations*. Edited by E. Cannan. New York: The Modern Library, 1937.

Spiegel, Henry W. *The Growth of Economic Thought*. Englewood Cliffs, N.J.: Prentice Hall, 1971. See pp. 216–20 for a brief discussion of Steuart, pp. 299–301 and pp. 302–6 for Sismondi, and pp. 352–4 for Senior.

Wieser, Friedrich von. *Social Economics*. Translated by A. F. Hinrichs. New York: Adelphi, 1927.

Chapter Three

Humanistic Economic Tradition

If the mathematical/scientific story were the only one to relate, economics would have strayed far from Adam Smith's understanding and telling. But in fact few economists accept that a quantitative account alone portrays today's or any earlier period's economic thinking. Most would concede validity to the following:

> Mainstream economics is widely recognized to have sacrificed a broad understanding of human nature for a restrictive model of *ratio*-nal behavior tailored to the requirements of a supply-and-demand [i.e., mathematical] explanation of the market process. Thus social scientists and humanists often bemoan the narrowness of contemporary mainstream economics, arguing that economists abstract from all that is interesting and difficult to explain in human behavior because it does not fit *rational* choice theory. [emphasis added] (Davis and O'Boyle 1994, 183)

Most economists, of course, take for granted that economic agents are persons seeking to gain the means needed for living and thereby their ultimate purpose in life, however they conceive it. They must suppose, therefore, that human persons, when placing economic acts, engage their powers of mind, will, heart, and senses, all of which are essential for every one of life's phases from the most exalted endeavors to grubbing for survival. In short, they implicitly agree that economic praxis, while necessarily quantitative, calls for analysis from a personal and humanistic perspective. The economic agent is not a rational automaton but, while tested in the crucible of economic rationality, is as multidimensional as life itself. From the beginning and paralleling the growth of economic science, scholars have detected and developed a humanistic tradition simply making what is implicit in the science explicit.

Even though the great leap forward in scientific empirical analysis started economic thinking on a new path away from the largely ethical concerns of scholars of business up to and into the eighteenth century, a steady stream of social scientists continued to think and write within the older tradition. In other words, while the quantitative and mathematical compose the major theme of modern theoretical economics, the personalist and humanistic minor theme was and still is orchestrated. There are many scholars, economists in particular, who are still much concerned about persons' material needs, employment, earning, gaining, and the moral and social implications of the same.

HUMANISTIC THEMES

The enormous literature of this genre of economic analysis cannot be presented exhaustively in just a few pages. Sampling this scholarship, beginning with a bit from the nineteenth century and continuing with a scattering from England, the Continent, and the United States up to today, will have to do. Even so most of the authors cited will be of recent and American vintage and only their most representative contributions acknowledged. And for anyone mentioned, there are ten or twelve who could well have been named.

While most of the scholars cited will not be in the economic mainstream, those who have achieved universal recognition have done so by developing the preter-economic side of the economic person. They have precedence in being listed here, not because their contributions are considered more important, but because their acceptance into the mainstream suggests their greater influence in causing economists, scholars of business, and practitioners to become uneasy about an exclusive quantitative emphasis and to encourage those already so inclined to intensify their interests in the humanistic and personalist aspects of economics.

One of the first so recognized is the sociologist/economist, Max Weber (1857–1929), whose *Theory of Social and Economic Organization* incorporated sociological and especially religious motivation into people's economic life, in particular presenting Reformation freethinking as basic to economic liberalism. R. H. Tawney (1880–1962) perceived this religious factor differently. He criticized the Protestant ethic for rationalizing the egocentrism which underlies capitalism, thereby transforming it into an acquisitive society. Karl Polanyi (1886–1964), in *The Great Transformation,* further condemned the market economy, seeing it as changed from a system of morally bonded relations, providing for personal material needs, to a structure *disembedded* from society and designed for individual gain seeking. Much like earlier scholars, Polanyi and Tawney were quite conscious of the moral implications in getting and spending.

From them to Thorstein Veblen's (1857–1929) institutionalism is a natural transition. With his first and most popular book, *The Theory of the Leisure*

Class, in the sardonic style unique to him and in the light of natural morality, he critiqued economic institutions and peoples' economic habits by which they use material goods to further their life's purposes. John R. Commons (1862–1945) then fashioned the philosophic foundations of institutionalism as well as the economics of the New Deal. In his *Institutional Economics* he argued that collective action, even as state intervention, can increase the liberty and effectiveness of private action. This concept in turn became part of the philosophic core later used to extol 'redistributive welfarism' as a more benevolent form of capitalism which in fact reflects secular vestiges of spiritual poverty.

Quite in another direction Joseph A. Schumpeter (1883–1950) analyzed the disruptive creativity of free enterprise. Especially in his *The Theory of Economic Development* and his *Capitalism, Socialism, and Democracy* he saw entrepreneurial innovation as a creative force. At the same time he acknowledged that innovation's dynamism tends to render obsolete older competing systems. It also generates the tendencies of large-scale enterprise to sap the sense of private property and to weaken the social framework that supports capitalistic enterprise. John M. Clark's (1884–1963) *Social Control of Business* is more optimistic that social controls and private freedom can be balanced by means of workable, i.e., effective and socially acceptable, competition. In this way, he argued, competition's dynamism is preserved and social welfare advanced. Like Clark and Schumpeter, Kenneth Boulding (1910–93) was a past president of the American Economic Association. From his first book, *The Reconstruction of Economics*, until his last, *The Future: Images and Processes*, coauthored with his wife, he ranged over the moral and social sciences, revealing their implications for economic thinking. A provocative speaker, he was a favorite at conferences devoted to humanistic and social economics.

Such gatherings are mostly attended by scholars who perceive economics in a holistic sense. Their interests usually proceed from three foci of concern, illustrated in the first chapter: religious beliefs, philosophic views, and pragmatic social experience. Belief in a Supreme Being and a personal final destiny, implying a moral mandate to do what is good and right for people, espouses justice, moderation, and charity as values in seeking and sharing wealth. A philosophic view of humanity, by espousing personhood as an individual's ultimate dignity and worth, judges economic actions according to how they enhance or degrade people as persons. Last, the pragmatic social approach evaluates economic conduct, policies, and institutions according to what experience affirms works in producing and distributing wealth in a socially effective way.

Though coming from different levels may spark disputes, the three approaches corroborate more than conflict. Both religious and philosophic convictions, while differing on other points, agree that economic persons, being set in and limited by time and space, must exist and act physically and so achieve their ends more easily in a peaceful and harmonious socioeconomic climate. In a pragmatic sense both approaches underscore that all economic acts must be tested in the crucible of justice. Conversely, effective institutions and social organizations must be judged by what is the dignity, worth, and ultimate destiny of persons. In sum, each focus is necessary; each supports the others and in turn is supported by them; each qualifies the others and in turn is qualified by them. An economist, while interested mainly in one area, will often be influenced by inferences from other perspectives.

As a consequence, scholars who work the humanistic and personalist halls of economic science will tend to slide from one approach to another. This makes for a rich, variegated, and changing tapestry but it also adds to the difficulty of synthesizing the field. As of now the humanistic approach to economics is wanting an Adam Smith or Alfred Marshall, a genius who can organize an enormous body of studies with their different approaches into a synoptic picture, producing what Schumpeter calls the "classical moment." What follows, though not comprehensive, will I hope illuminate a body of economic studies deserving of more public attention. In any case, the three foci will serve to organize the chapter.

THE RELIGIOUS FOCUS

Of these the richest is that nourished by religious beliefs, which generate both social action and social theory and are able to mine the long tradition of moral literature back through Modern, Medieval, and Biblical times. In the United States the former was more evident than the latter up into this century. The Social Gospel movement, born from pre-Civil War Evangelism, was a "North American Protestant ecumenical effort to meet social concerns and reform economic life" (Ryan 1991, 517). Mainly a pulpit phenomenon, it gained scholarly stature by sharing the prestige of Richard T. Ely (1845–1943), a notable scholar and cofounder of the American Economic Association. From then to the present the Social Gospel has produced such a steady stream of biblical critique of contemporary economic theory and institutions as M. Douglas Meeks's *God the Economist* and Richard Niebanck's *Economic Justice*, treatises on how to incorporate Christian principles in one's economic and business practices. Some economists of this mind have belatedly formed the Association of Christian Economists.

By contrast, in Europe, more so on the Continent than England, theorists, heirs to a rich body of Social Philosophy and Social Theology going back to the Middle Ages, responded immediately to the secularizing trends of the nineteenth century. Scholars such as the Spaniard Ramon de la Sagra (1798–1871), the Italian Jesuit Matteo Liberatore (1810–92), Bishop Emmanuel von Ketteler of Mainz (1811–77), the Austrian Karl von Vogelsang (1818–90), and French René de la Tour du Pin (1834–1924), are but a handful of those who contributed to the discussions. Though drawing from the same tradition they differed ideologically from the woefully reactionary to the blatantly liberal. For all, contemporaneity was achieved only with effort.

From this same tradition the Vatican, starting with Leo XIII (1810–1903), also addressed the modern world and its scientific revolution in a continuous stream of social encyclicals: *Rerum Novarum* (1891), *Quadragesimo Anno* (1931), *Mater et Magistra* (1961), *Laborem Exercens* (1981), and *Centesimus Annus* (1991), to name but some of the most important for economic thought. Two principles are fundamental to and permeate this body of doctrine: the right of independent scientific inquiry and the obligation and, therefore, right of the Church and other moral authorities to enunciate ethical principles applicable to economic praxis.

Slowly and indeed reluctantly the voice of the Vatican came to be acknowledged as an authentic critique of modern industrial society. Some of its most basic humanistic and moral principles—the right to a family living income, the priority of the needs of the poor, the dignity of labor, the right to private property, the right to subordinate but free economic association, and, on the other hand, the right of the state to intervene in the economy for reasons of achieving justice—are a few of the principles that have become commonplace and generally accepted moral dicta within the general amorality of free enterprise economics.

Initially neither this European effort nor Leo XIII's encyclical caused much concern in the largely immigrant American Catholic Church, concerned more about poverty, education, and the rights of labor. But the publication of *Quadragesimo Anno* right in the middle of the Great Depression and especially also the teaching and writing of Msgr. John A. Ryan (1869–1945) jump-started the intellectual concerns of a group of Catholic economists into forming the Catholic Economic Association in 1941. Its professional character was set by the scholarly qualities of its founding committee. Thomas F. Divine, S.J., who did his graduate work under Lionel Robbins at the London School of Economics, was its first president and also editor of the *Review of Social Economy*. Other founding members, such as Harvard's Edward Chamberlin and Columbia's Raymond Saulnier, though differing on analytic matters, were united in their concern for a holistic approach to economic science, which saw the economic person as much a religious as a secular being.

Always, therefore, more ecumenical than its name, CEA in 1970 became the Association for Social Economics. Enlisting a membership whose interests ranged from Papal to Marxian social thought, ASE gleans a rich yield of research in and analysis of the humanistic side of economics from the liberation theology of a Gustavo Gutierrez to the defense of free-market economics of a Michael Novak. It was especially productive of scholars like Stephen Worland, George Rohrlich, and Arnold McKee, who, drawing from papal and other sources of social thought, criticized and mediated the ideas of a range of scholars, uncovering in their works inherent or implicit links to more explicit religious and moral traditions.

Some scholars—not necessarily those cited above—have been content to stay with a religious focus, taking the high road of moral principles as they apply to economic and business conduct, like the encyclicals and pastoral letters from various religious bodies. Others have followed such moral perspectives as leads into the nitty-gritty of empirical research. Of those who come to economic issues from a philosophic point of departure, some will blend in a religious focus. More numerous are those who combine two or more philosophic points of view. Some scholars will combine philosophic with sociological, psychological, or political theories. Only a few will proceed from a single point of philosophic departure. However the variations, this category of economic analysis is more complex than the previous.

THE PHILOSOPHIC APPROACH

In fact economists in this category, like their predecessors from the Modern, Scholastic, and Classical traditions, so combine the sources of their philosophic inspiration that there are almost as many categories as there are economists. Typical of the categorizing problem is classifying E. F. Schumacher (1911–77). Although he converted to Catholicism, his *Small is Beautiful: Economics as if People Mattered* reflects more Buddhist thought and Gandhian economics. Others will come from every point of the philosophic compass. Amitai Etzioni's *The Moral Dimension* derives from the Kantian categorical imperative a communitarian economic system. (A communitarian theme is the principal thrust of the Society for the Advancement of Socioeconomics which Etzioni was instrumental in founding in 1989.) Mark Lutz and Kenneth Lux, in recalling Sismondi's welfare deviations from Smith in their *Humanistic Economics: The New Challenge*, rather blend Maslow's list of human needs into Kantian thought as criteria to judge whether economic institutions foster human self-realization. More mainstream in intent, John J. Piderit's *The Ethical Foundations of Economics* adapts an empirically derived natural law ethics into neoclassical economic theory.

Tibor Scitovsky's *The Joyless Economy* probes deeply into the psychology of consumption by distinguishing between economic and personal satisfaction, arguing from empirical psychology that the amounts the economic person has and buys simply do not measure the comfort, stimulation, and pleasure goods can bring. With him should be listed two philosophers who have developed theories of general welfare and self-interest which have stirred the economic brotherhood.

John Rawls in his *A Theory of Justice* presumes a kind of Lockean social contract, distinctive of a nation's culture. From this he derives the ideal form of social justice by combining the most extensive personal freedom with such economic inequalities that no other arrangement would improve the welfare of those most in need. Robert Nozick harkens back to a more Hobbesian state of nature in which autonomous individuals possess inviolable rights to life, health, liberty, and property. While his *Anarchy, State, and Utopia* expresses the ultralibertarian ideas that egocentric utility determines action, a minimal state is sufficient to protect rights, and governments are needed to protect entitlements and to rectify past injustices.

Two philosophic approaches influenced enough scholars in the States to almost be called schools of economic thought. One is Clarence Ayres's (1891–1971) synthesis of Veblen's institutionalism with Dewey's instrumentalism. His *Theory of Economic Progress* sets down the fundamental principles that values are determined pragmatically by use and that material technology is the major influence on economic institutions and behavior. This approach inspires an agenda of empirical research and social criticism, which is centered in the Association of Evolutionary Economics, founded in 1963.

The other philosophic school, which numbers a substantial following, is a European import, the solidarist economics of the Jesuit Heinrich Pesch (1854–1926). Rupert Ederer has translated the five volumes of his *Lehrbuch der Nationaloekonomie* but it has only as yet been published in abbreviated form.[1] Pesch's works and his famous seminar influenced the industry council ideas of Pius XI as well as the policies of Konrad Adenauer's Christian Democrats in the reconstruction of the German economy after World War II.

The United States also benefited in that several of his students, Goetz Brief and Franz Mueller, for example, came to the United States after fleeing Nazi Germany. Their teaching and writing have been a consistent stimulant of solidarist thinking to a new generation of American scholars.

Solidarism derives from the basic intuition that people are socially interdependent and indeed need each other. In economic matters it implies a mutual justice in exchange, a just sharing in contributing to and gaining from production, and, above all, a concern for the common good (Waters 1993, 277–8). In the United States the specifically American version of solidarism is owing largely to Bernard W. Dempsey, S.J. (1903–60). From an initial and lasting interest in papal thought, Dempsey went on to Harvard to study under Schumpeter and did extensive reading of the Jesuit scholastic philosophers,

Molina, Lessius, and de Lugo. Thus, his several books and many articles were richly textured by both an incisive grasp of current money, labor, capital, and product markets and by a clear presentation of the principles of cooperation, community, and social justice. From these insights he demonstrates how a functioning, effective, and beneficial economic system could be achieved. His impress on students and other social economists, despite an untimely death, was lasting.

Josef Solterer was one who always acknowledged Dempsey's influence. Though coming late both to the United States and to academia, Solterer, as a charter member of CEA-ASE, devoted a half-century to studying and writing about the role of justice in guiding the dynamics of economic action and innovation. With his last work, "The Economics of Justice," which integrates and summarizes six or so previous articles, he adapted justice to the dynamics of the economic process. As a virtuous habit, justice not only guides the stream of individual exchanges in generating values and incomes but it also monitors those transforming innovations that change the economy's course. This pattern of recurrence and adaptation Solterer sees as replicating all phases of human reality, from the external universe of matter and energy to the internal world of intuition and thought and then to the galaxy of cognitive constructs which persons use to express their grasp of reality and to service their needs: number systems and mathematics, languages and literatures, tunes and compositions, and, in the economic order, values, capital, and wealth. This brilliant summary of a life's scholarly effort fittingly went to press on the day Josef Solterer (1897–1991) died.

The tragic sublimity of a Dempsey's or Solterer's career has been repeated in unnumbered variations throughout the academic world and amongst social economists specifically, because for the most part they labored with at best the faintest acknowledgment. No Nobel Prize theirs. Very frequently they are castigated along with the most narrow-minded mathematicizers by scholars from the moral and social sciences, the very ones who should be looking out for allies among the sons and daughters of Adam Smith.

THE PRAGMATIC SOCIAL APPROACH

In an even more anomalous way are the social economists, who research the institutions, laws, policies, cultures, and values, which impact on economic persons' activities: their patterns of consumption, employment, working conditions, management skills, and philosophies, and, of course, their relations to government. All such reflect gender, race, morals, religion, personal drive, social skills, education, and material well-being of persons in their diverse economic roles. Economic acts being quantitative, these factors can be empirically observed and correlated to buying and selling, hiring and firing, saving and investing, and all the rest. In other words, economic action is part and parcel of one's social, cultural, and political life. Thus pragmatic economists have an unlimited agenda of empirical and quantitative research, which still reflects a personal and humanistic point of view and can be applied to conduct.

Pragmatic social research, therefore, includes an extensive range of interests from studying factors generating individual economic actions to considerations of cultural, racial, or other generic differences that affect economic institutions and then on to purely mathematical and theoretical analysis. Hence, a limit must be set somewhere. Here it is arbitrarily set at studies which deal principally with those factors and conditions which affect or influence personal conduct. Admittedly, therefore, much important institutional research will not be included here.

As one expects, therefore, many scholars come to this social economic agenda with neither religious nor philosophic focus but with just an intuition that the human factors, which distinguish classes of people or even individuals and the economic roles they play, are significant for one's utility preferences and consequent economic choices. Conversely, scholars who approach such empirical research with a perception of human life-purposes and a clear idea of the nature and dignity of human beings, will be able to frame their conclusions in ways that make them more relevant to economic persons' conduct in their actual daily dealings and relations with each other.

One scholar who does this exemplarily is Edward J. O'Boyle. His writing on worker/employer cooperation, poverty, health care costs, employment, and homelessness clearly delineate both courses of right action for daily living and principles for public policy. All of this he casts in a framework of *Personalist Economics* (1998).

Jonathan Boswell begins somewhat differently by blending the three social values of liberty, equality, and fraternity, each modifying and focusing the others, but so harmonized as to generate democratic communitarianism. This, he then shows by empirical and historical examples, is buttressed by the social structures of continuity, appropriate size, openness to public scrutiny, and close working relationships (Boswell 1990).

Reversing this process, David Ellerman from his many years of studying the Mondragon and other cooperative forms has now, in his *Property and Contract in Economics,* formulated a new theory of economic democracy. Essentially he rejects the ordinary labor contract as a kind of slavery, proposing instead what he calls a labor theory of property, which he asserts is fundamental to and leads to economic democracy. Severyn Bruyn, having spent years researching economic institutions as human alignments that are socially rooted and managed, manifests a like scholarly pattern. His latest book, *A Future for the American Economy: The Social Market*, universalizes this concept into a general theory of self-regulating markets producing a social and democratic economy. He is thus thoroughly solidaristic in spirit (Waters 1994, 119).

Gunnar Myrdal's (1898–1987) *An American Dilemma* tends to be more pessimistic. Not only does he expose the contradiction in Americans' believing in universal human equality while accepting unequal genetic status, but he demonstrates how such racial prejudice cumulatively confirms the contradiction by aggravating the economic disparity among peoples. From a like existential contrariety, J. R. Stanfield has sought "experientially authenticated knowledge" to resolve the conflict between real individual freedom expressed in self-interest and those collective interests which keep society going. Hence his scholarship tends toward explaining how the interaction between societal and individual economics can be mutually beneficial (Stanfield 1986).

Others have a more specific social economic agenda. Walter Adams, on his own and more recently with James Brock, has pointed out the deleterious effects of corporate gigantism and unfettered mergers and buyouts. Related to this, William Dugger has almost single-mindedly focused his empirical studies and interests on the corporate culture of managing for profits only, which the teaching of contemporary economic science tends to entrench. The husband-and-wife team of Larry Alan Bear and Rita Maldanado-Bear, in their *Free Markets, Finance, Ethics, and Law*, argue that public and personal values must be expressed in laws which so regulate corporate and bureaucratic behavior as to inculcate a sense of public stewardship.

Another set of economists including Herman Daly, Douglas Booth, Georgescu-Roegen, among others, have researched the problems of economic growth and environmental deterioration. Nor can one pass over the thousands of technicians and specialists in government and private agencies who gather and collate the economic and related data that is the stuff of research.

In short, the catalogue is almost endless of economists who occasionally or regularly address such social factors as education, moral principles, politics, gender, race, and poverty, which impact somehow on economic persons' conduct and utility preferences. Apologies are certainly due to the hundreds of contemporary and thousands of past economists, who have materially contributed to a humanistic economics but are not mentioned. The random and somewhat haphazard listing of those who are cited can hardly give a comprehensive and accurate picture of contemporary and earlier economic studies of this nature which have been generated in the United States and worldwide. But the wide range of perspectives on and paths to such studies does demonstrate that concern for a humanistic tradition in economic science is not only valid but flourishing and growing.

Recalling this and the previous chapters does reveal a basic theme that the business of producing, exchanging, and using goods and services is essential for human personal living. Obvious to and practiced by all for millennia prior to historical time, economics as science, as a mathematical and quantitative process, only became of interest to scholars relatively recently in time. Beginning with Greek intellectualism, the economic elements of living were of some concern to a few of the most learned, Plato, Aristotle, Cicero, Aquinas, and others, analyzing its implications for moral living, family well-being, political stability, or just establishing one's state in life. As scholars delved deeper into the problems of managing one's material welfare, it became evident that all economic activity coalesces into a vast societal enterprise.

This point is dramatized by simply contrasting the English manorial economy of a millennium ago with national/global economies today. Then the economic orbit of most people was concentrated in what could be gathered, grown, or fabricated on the manor itself, with occasional sales at regional markets and purchase from wandering peddlers. Such economies seldom provide more than survival means for the peasants, somewhat more for the lord and his retinue, and a small tribute to the suzerain. Its functioning was simplicity itself; its growth barely perceptible; comprehending it no problem.

By contrast, in national and global economies today the flood of scientific facts generate new products, new productive methods, new means and ways of financing, and new government and legal regulations, all in constant process, all driven by the desires of economic persons, taken together, to improve their material well-being. This in itself takes no mean skill to understand the complex interworkings of a modern economy even without politicians' meddling to "improve" it.

At that stage, obviously, economics must be seen as a science like the natural sciences: empirical, quantitative, generalized, contingent, and secular. Indeed the economics that economists learn is a kind of esoteric wisdom, acquired only after years of study. But economics never became a science whose elegance is a joy in, of, and for itself but whose purpose is to rationalize persons' material actions. Even so the vast majority of people know little of scientific economics, yet do well enough in managing their economic affairs.

Nevertheless, as tooled knowledge, economics has the practical purpose of transforming scientific principles into standards and guides which enhance material living. But at the same time it must be granted that, given its wealth-creating possibilities, economics can contribute to conduct which demeans people, fragments society, and creates instruments destructive of both people and environments. Taken together these considerations imply the need to look beyond treating economics as analysis, as just an empirical and quantitative science, to seeing it as a praxis, acts and habits which are subject to moral criteria.

Given economists' training in and predilection for empirical analysis, it may be conceded that the quantitative is and should be the dominant mode of economic science. Nevertheless, one may insist on the pragmatic behavioral functions of economics itself. This is confirmed in that its first name from the Greek '*oikonomikos*,' meaning household management, has stuck with the science instead of more elegant scientific names like 'catallactics'—the science of exchanges—or 'chrematistics'—the science of wealth.

Thus economics' history yields two conclusions. First, many people and scholars besides professional economists are rightly concerned about economic matters as an inherent condition for human living and welfare. Second, economics like other social sciences has a humanistic side, dealing with peoples' cultures, relationships, institutions, values, and aspirations, which must be taken into account. The quantitative and the humanitarian may contend for scholars' interest and effort but neither cancels the other: economic reality is simply incomplete without both.

This is not to imply, as some economists do, that economics is a moral science in the strict sense of moral: as what is right or wrong for the human person's ultimate good and purpose. Rather, what is meant here is that economic acts are both *moral and economic*. They are economic in that they are necessary means for persons to act and survive. At the same time the acts are moral or immoral insofar as they relate to dealing justly with other people and in using material things as means to their ultimate good and purpose. Thus economics is both a praxis and a science and therefore, its polarities: the quantitative/mathematical and the behavioral/social. As a science it is like other sciences, morally neutral, simply a body of knowledge and principles which may be correct or incorrect but not morally right or wrong. As a praxis, however, a doing or making by human persons, economic acts or economic conduct may be judged as simply successful or failing but they can also be judged unjust, imprudent, intemperate, and in general moral or immoral.

The further study, therefore, becomes part of the current agenda of emphasizing the personal aspects of economic activity. By analyzing some of the foundational economic concepts, processes, and institutions in the light of personalist principles, it hopes in a modest way to contribute to what others have brought so far forward. It proceeds from the most basic idea that, while all economic acts involve ratios of quantities gained and given, these acts are placed by economic persons. Hence, what economic persons are, what distinguishes them from other material beings, and what elements of their nature are relevant to their economic lives are questions important for right economic conduct.

So this short survey of past economic thinking and analysis says that economic theory was culled from economic practice and that economic analysis and economic praxis, while distinguishable in theory, are inseparable in fact.

All in all, therefore, understanding the economy today requires not only technical analytical skills but a good understanding of the nature of economic agents, the people who consume, produce, market, finance, and innovate economic goods and services. That calls for examining how the tradition of economic humanism is fulfilled in analysis of the economic agent as the Economic Person.

NOTES

1. The complete translation of Pesch's *Lehrbuch* is currently being published by The Edwin Mellen Press.

REFERENCES

Adams, Walter, and J. W. Brock. *Dangerous Pursuits: Mergers and Acquisitions in the Age of Wall Street*. New York: Pantheon, 1989.

Ayres, C. E. *Theory of Economic Progress: A Study in the Fundamentals of Economic Development and Culture*. New York: Schocken, 1962.

Bear, Larry Alan, and Rita Maldanado-Bear. *Free Markets, Finance. Ethics, and Law*. Englewood Cliffs, N.J.: Prentice Hall, 1993.

Boulding, Kenneth. *A Reconstruction of Economics*. New York: John Wiley & Sons, 1950.

Boulding, Kenneth, and Elise Boulding. *The Future: Images and Processes*. Thousand Oaks, Calif.: Sage, 1995.

Boswell, Jonathan. *Community and the Economy: The Theory of Public Co-operation*. New York: Routledge, 1990.

Bruyn, Severyn T. *A Future for the American Economy: The Social Market*. Stanford, Calif.: Stanford University Press, 1991.

Clark, John M. *Social Control of Business*. Chicago: University of Chicago Press, 1926.

Commons, J. R. *Institutional Economics: Its Place in Political Economy*. New York: Macmillan, 1934.

Davis, John B., and Edward J. O'Boyle. "Reconstruction of Mainstream Economics and the Market Ecomomy." *The Social Economics of Human Material Need*. Carbondale, Ill.: Southern Illinois University Press, 1994: 182–209.

Dempsey, Bernard. W., S.J. *The Functional Economy: The Bases of Economic Organization*. Englewood Cliffs, N.J.: Prentice Hall, 1958.

Dugger, William. *Underground Economics: A Decade of Institutionalist Dissent*. Armonk, N.Y.: M. E. Sharpe, 1992.

Ederer, Rupert. "Heinrich Pesch, Solidarity, and Social Encyclicals." *Review of Social Economy* 49, no. 4 (1991): 596–610.

Ellerman, David. *Property and Contract in Economics: The Case for Economic Democracy*. Malden, Mass.: Blackwell, 1992.

Etzioni, Amitai. *The Moral Dimension: Toward a New Economics*. New York: Free Press, 1988.

John XXIII. *Mater et Magistra (Christianity and Social Progress)*. New York: America Press, 1961.

John Paul II. *Laborem Exercens (On Human Work)*. Boston: St. Paul Editions, 1981.

——. *Centesimus Annus: The Encyclicals in Everyday Language*. Danders, N.Y.: Orbis, 1996.

Leo XIII. "The Condition of Labor: Five Great Encyclicals." *Rerum Novarum*. New York: Paulist Press: 1891.

Lutz, Mark A., and Kenneth Lux. *Humanistic Economics: The New Challenge*. New York: The Bootstrap Press, 1988.

Meeks, M. Douglas. *God the Economist: The Doctrine of God and Political Economy*. Minneapolis, Minn.: Fortress, 1989.

Myrdal, Gunnar. *An American Dilemma: The Negro Problem and Modern Democracy*. New York: Harper & Row, 1944.

Niebanck, Richard J. *Economic Justice: An Evangelical Perspective*. Christian Social Responsibility Series. New York: Division For Mission in North America, Lutheran Church in America, 1980.

Nozick, Robert. *Anarchy, State, and Utopia*. New York: Basic Books, 1974.

O'Boyle, Edward J. "Homo Socio-Economicus: Foundational to Social Economics and Social Economy." *Review of Social Economy* 52, no. 3 (1994): 286–313.

——. *Personalist Economics: Moral Convictions, Economic Realities, and Social Action*. Boston: Kluwer, 1998.

Piderit, John J., S.J. *The Ethical Foundations of Economics*. Washington, D.C.: Georgetown University Press, 1993.

Pius XI. "Reconstructing the Social Order." *Five Great Encyclicals*. New York: Paulist Press, 1931.

Polanyi, Karl. *The Great Transformation*. Boston: Beacon Press, 1957.

Rawls, John. *A Theory of Justice*. Cambridge, Mass: Harvard University Press, 1971.

Ryan, Leo V., C. S. V. "American Protestant and Catholic Social Concerns circa 1890 and the Ely-Ryan Relationship." *Review of Social Economy* 49, no. 4 (1991): 514–31.

Schumacher, E. F. *Small is Beautiful: Economics as if People Mattered*. New York: Harper & Row, 1973.

Schumpeter, Joseph A. *Capitalism, Socialism, and Democracy*. New York: Harper & Row, 1942.

——. *History of Economic Analysis*. Edited from manuscript by E. B. Schumpeter. New York: Oxford University Press, 1954.

Scitovsky, Tibor. *The Joyless Economy: An Inquiry into Human Satisfaction and Consumer Dissatisfaction*. New York: Oxford University Press, 1976.

Seligman, Ben B. *Main Currents in Modern Economics: Economic Thought Since 1870*. New York: Free Press of Glencoe, 1962.

Solterer, Josef. "The Economics of Justice." *Review of Social Economy* 49, no. 4 (1991): 559–65.

Stanfield, J. R. *Economic Thought and Social Change*. Carbondale, Ill.: Southern Illinois University Press, 1979.

——. *The Economic Thought of Karl Polanyi: Lives and Livelihood*. London: Macmillan: New York: St. Martin's, 1986.

Tawney, R. H. *The Acquisitive Society*. New York: Harcourt, Brace, and Howe, 1920.

Veblen, Thorstein. *The Theory of the Leisure Class: An Economic Study of Institutions.* New York: Mentor Books, 1953.

Waters, William R. "A Review of the Troops: Social Economics in the Twentieth Century," *Review of Social Economy* 51, no. 3 (1993): 262–85.

———. "A Solidarist Social Economy: The Bruyn Perspective," *Review of Social Economy* 52, no. 1 (1994): 108–21.

Weber, Max. *The Theory of Social and Economic Organization.* Translated by A. M. Henderson and Talcott Parsons. New York: Oxford University Press, 1947.

Chapter Four

Economic Personalism

Alfred Marshall, who—more than anyone—fashioned economic science's mathematical format, saw economists' role as being more than just technical proficiency; "The progress of men's nature," he writes, "is the ultimate aim of economic studies" (Marshall 1961, 75). Few economists, and none of the most famous, cavil at this. As shown earlier, a steady stream of scholars have investigated the moral and other social sciences for insights into the nature, psyche, patterns of acting, institutions, and cultures of economic agents. Seeing them from a human/social aspect opened economic thought to a host of real-life considerations. I propose here and in the following chapters to examine economic agents as persons and what personhood implies for economic acts.

'Person' is derived from the Latin *per sonans*, 'sounding through,' referring to the masks players in classic drama wore, serving to identify, express, and externalize the character which is portrayed and to project the actor's voice. A person, therefore, is what a human being is, what he or she perceives when affirming "*I am*." A person knows self without an intermediary, immediately, directly, and absolutely. A person is aware of self and aware of being aware. Being self-aware, persons can express themselves by sound, light, action, and in even more esoteric ways.

That sets the agenda for this chapter. Persons do economics, buying and selling, producing, saving, investing, and so on. Persons are economic agents in concert with others who are also economic agents. Conveniently, then, one needs only examine one's dealings with others to see how economic agents act. The chapter, therefore, will address three questions: What does personhood mean and entail? What does a life-career as person imply? Why and how do persons conduct their economic affairs?

THE HUMAN PERSON

About persons, no one says it better than Emmanuel Mounier, "The person is not the most marvelous object in the world, nor anything else that we can know from the outside. It is the one reality that we know, and . . . are at the same time fashioning from within" (Mounier 1952, xviii).[1] A person's affirmation, "I am," therefore, states the most certain empirical fact possible, since to doubt or deny it is to affirm it. Indeed, every statement of fact, speculation, belief, or opinion reaffirms the existence of the affirmer. In short, it is the empirical rock upon which a personalist view of humankind is based. Conclusions drawn from it, therefore, share in its certitude.

That does not say that persons know themselves accurately and fully, but only that the observing subject is identical with the object observed. Nor does it suggest that most people are aware of their personhood, but it does imply that doing so will reveal some of the essential wonders of being human.

First, to see one's self as person is to realize immediately that as person one exists not only subjectively but bodily; that is, a human person is an *embodied self-consciousness and knows body in knowing self*. The human person as self-knowing, that is, the knower as the known, is indeed wholly spirit. But since in this life a person cannot know without being nor be without body, the body is essential, not just an appendage, a burden, or something of embarrassment. Bodies are the instruments by which persons express themselves, and the only way they can act, whether jackhammering concrete or composing a concerto. Even better: persons by being embodied escape "the solitude of a thinking that would be only thought about thought " (Mounier 1952, 11).

A body can be defective: impaired from birth, become more or less gravely diseased, incur disabilities, and at last will stop functioning. Nevertheless, human persons do not have bodies but are wholly body, just as they are wholly spirit. Nothing affirms this better than examples of those disabled or seriously ill who marshal other spiritual and physical powers and resources to overcome their impairments. Such proclaim that a person is the one and essential I: an embodied reflexive consciousness.

Second, every person is unique but yet related to all other persons. As the product of two distinct genetic histories, each person carries a unique DNA code. (The exceptions are identical twins who, nevertheless, can be individuated by time and place.) Moreover, when the sperm fertilizes the ovum it relates this singular future person to parents, their other children and their kindred, neighbors, schoolmates, colleagues, and others. Thus, the very process which individuates persons also forms linkages with the entire human race. Individuality and sociality are not contradictories but polarities of the same personalist continuum.

As such, personhood must be distinguished from selfhood. That is, while personhood implies self-awareness, it is not of a self cocooned within itself but of a self whose very being relates to and depends on other persons and is depended on by others. Selfhood is self-regarding and narcissistic; personhood is open to needs and inviting of others.

Third, personhood, the wonderful nature humans possess, is shared by all. Persons are equal by nature. But they are differentiated and individuated by their bodily sizes and shapes and by the development of their organs, nervous systems, muscles, and other characteristics. Consequently, people differ in size, strength, speed, alertness, sensitivity, and every other way by their physical endowments as these, in turn, are affected by environment and governed by their physical and organic development. All of this implies a process of continuous change in place and over time.

Persons, however, are not defined by when or where they are. Quite the contrary, persons through all life's phases and ever-changing physical circumstances know themselves as substantial unities which survive, "perduring through all of the vicissitudes of change and chance and choice" (Kavanaugh 1994, 16). A baby at the breast is the same as will be the grandmother dozing before the fire. As baby she is not just potentially human but a human with potentials and just so she will be through all life's phases and actuations of her possibilities. This, the basic unity of every person, as each grows and unfolds from diverse experiences over time, bestows both sight and hindsight, which together produce foresight. This ability to foresee what consequences a set of events and facts is likely to produce helps persons steer around undesirable inevitabilities a course of action might impose. As such, foresight is essential to the human person's moral freedom.

Freedom and Morality

Personal freedom and morality are as necessarily paired as male and female. While realizing marital bliss 'ever after' is promised only in fairy tales and the masculine/feminine union is no guarantee of peaceful coexistence, still almost all take the chance and most do well enough to prove that gender pairing is natural. So, too, freedom and morality, although often seeming at odds and actually at times difficult to square, mutually support each other. Freedom implies no or few restraints on a person's being and action, while morality requires seeking one's own good and helping others achieve their good as persons. That is, freedom pertains to the manner of a person's acting and morality to its real and final purpose. Some clarification will help.

The appetites for sex, wealth, food, and drink, for example, while intended to serve persons' ultimate good, can subvert them by seeking immediate pleasures. But a truly free person is not controlled by appetites and passions but employs and enjoys them as means to his or her final end. Likewise, the individual person, in being linked to others, may find that others' good constrain one's own. But seeing others as persons requires understanding their good as both essential to them and producing a closer union mutually beneficial to both. Finally, both freedom's magnet and the ultimate good's lure combine to preserve personal unity against the dissipating effects of time and change. Above all, despite life's constant process of physical, social, and experiential change, a true sense of freedom does not revoke but reinforces a person's intuition of essential unity and purpose.

Thus a person's capacity for freedom is not just being clear of restraints. Freedom is not "just a hiatus in the sequence of determinism" but "an affirmation of the person" (Mounier 1952, 54). Freedom is the freedom of a person, an embodied spirit situated in the world, a part of nature, conditioned and limited by the laws of the society to which it belongs. In short, a person is neither an encapsulated ego or an autonomous being; therefore, human freedom requires, first of all, accepting and basing one's conduct on the fact that not everything is possible.

But more fundamental to freedom is the moral conviction that persons as self-knowing and self-affirming beings can acknowledge their acts and accept responsibility for them. Furthermore, they can exercise choice—the ability to prefer one person, one thing, one action over another—and in so doing they are really choosing themselves. In sum, the essence of freedom does not consist in exemption from care and restraint, in indeterminism, or in doing nothing, but in acting as self-seeing beings who are responsible for their own conduct. As the very condition of personhood, the exercise of freedom is the practice of morality. "The center and pivot of freedom . . . lies in the progressive liberation to choose the good" (Mounier 1952, 63).

The individual person's unique freedom, therefore, means that each person is irreplaceable at the time and in the place he or she occupies. While related to others, each person is in some important ways a being on its own, not inhering in another; each person is a universe, an end in and for self. In this most basic sense, each is also a moral being. In knowing self, others, and the world, a person can question and evaluate everything. Knowing one's actions as one's own, a person can acknowledge and accept them as embodying and expressing one's self. They manifest one's personal reality and thus reveal one's intentions and moral life. The basic dignity of human persons consists in their being free, moral, and self-responsible beings. Kavanaugh is to the point:

I relate to my actions as my own. I know them as of me and by me. When I act, I am not merely regurgitating internalized information. As a centered consciousness I can make affirmations in and through them. My actions embody and express me, what I am, who I am. They are self-revelations. They reveal my personal reality, my self-consciously chosen intention, my moral life. (1994, 13)

Personhood, let it be emphasized, is not the dignity of some super being, an autonomous and isolated ego, but of a vulnerable creature who acknowledges frailty and moral and physical evil. He or she is not free of gender, culture, history, and race, and acknowledges it. To the contrary, in truly accepting personhood a person knows it as the vulnerable reality of a mortal being, whose 'comeuppance' now and again is salutary. Personal dignity, therefore, is not a thing of the person's own making but largely a gift one honors and obeys. It is the concept and conviction of moral responsibility which a person must cultivate through life's course and career. In sum, "To be a person is to be an expressive agent, a self-creating drama, a center of action, a narrative conscious of itself" (Kavanaugh 1994, 14).

PERSONHOOD AS DRAMA AND CAREER

In truth, human morality has the texture and the ingredients of drama. As an embodied self-consciousness, personhood is best portrayed in a career of self-development, the effort and action of becoming personal by blending contraries: spirit/body, male/female, individual/social, self-aware yet reaching out, unified but constantly changing, free but morally restrained. As human history repeatedly affirms, persons' struggles with the dilemmas of contraries involve the conflict between the forces of personalization and depersonalization.

In this drama, most basic and frequent is the downward pull of matter, a sensuality, which puts pleasure before purpose even to the point where sense gratification becomes an addiction and eventually a dehumanizing vice. But more ruinous than sensuality is a self-absorbing individualism. Becoming an ideology, it so isolates people and makes them so distrustful of each other that they lose a sense of their own personhood by disregarding that of others. Worst are the superegoists, who exploit others just as means in their arrogant striving for wealth, fame, and power. By belittling and trampling on others' personhood they extirpate their own and thus sink to the lowest level of depersonalization. Witness Buchenwald and the Gulag Archipelago! But even persons who are normally decent may find it difficult to treat others always as the persons they are and never in a depersonalized way.

As drama, therefore, striving to fulfill a personal destiny requires a triangulated effort: the values a person espouses are important both in forming one's *moral outlook and character* and in setting one's *relations with others*. This is especially so of a deep and operative conviction of both one's own and others' dignity as human persons. Such is a dialectic process in which a greater respect for others' personhood produces deeper understanding of one's own. Contrarily, preferring lower values to it not only corrodes conviction of the dignity of oneself and others as persons, but often generates moral tragedy. Macbeth's lust for the crown drove him not only to kill his king, alienate friends, and pervert his wife, but made him so superstitious and paranoid as to erode both military judgment and royal command.

In this moral drama and career, therefore, of all the values a person may espouse the value of personhood is key. Perceiving oneself as self-knowing and self-judging, as responsible, free and capable of love and of assuming another's good as one's own, these constitute a person's dignity (Kavanaugh 1994, 20) and are the basic elements of the value-person. Internalizing this value, therefore, not only becomes a dominant guide to conduct, around which other values collect, but perceiving the same value in the neighbor is to initiate movement toward others as essentially the same as oneself, thus seeing them as social and cooperative.

Consequently, of all the elements of the personal career and human drama one might examine, the two most relevant to seeing how personalism relates to economics will be, first, to review how values are espoused and the value hierarchy formed. Second, the value-person will then be analyzed in light of the dialectic between perceiving the value in others and a deeper experience of one's own personhood, both fostering community and collaboration. (But first note that the discussion will be about personal values by which a person lives and not about economic values for which one trades.)

Values and the Value Hierarchy

People form values from perceiving and preferring qualities of things, self, others, and relations among things and persons as good in themselves and of worth for acting and life.[2] How self, others, and things appear as good, therefore, becomes the critical question, because everything encountered can be perceived under any one, several or all modalities of good to bad: pleasing to painful, useful to useless, vital to lifeless, beautiful to ugly, true to false, right to wrong, holy to evil. Value modalities, in turn, are ranked by evidencing the four value criteria: basic, enduring, fulfilling, and integral, sense values being the least endowed and spiritual and sacred values the most. Therefore, the modalities by which a person primarily and regularly perceives reality measure his or her moral state. Sensualists are prone to see and to choose on the basis of pleasure or pain; the more spiritually minded on the truth or rightness of their choices.

But forming a value hierarchy, one's complex of operative values, is never final nor a neat and tidy task, reflecting as it does a person's culture, temperament, circumstances, and life vicissitudes. Indeed, a person may often unwittingly hold contradictory dominant values. Whatever the state of one's value system—proceeding to become a true hierarchy, mired in sensual values or just dormant—the values one espouses manifest one's moral life. The more a person penetrates into the good of self, others, and things, the higher the value modalities one realizes. "'Values by illuminating others', as well as one's own, goodness, become both guides and goals of conduct" (Danner 1994, 90).

Espoused values, therefore, are more than moral benchmarks. A person lives and acts by the values one espouses and especially by one's dominant values, about which lesser ones gather; values are like searchlights, pointing the way not just to avoid trouble but to engage life, to confront the world by accepting a sense of personal responsibility, and to bring people together. Therefore, cultivating and espousing the most basic, enduring, absolute, and spiritual values is more than fighting against matter's downward pull and wanting pleasure and ease. It is to choose a career of purifying oneself of a self-centered individualism and defending values worth dying for, if necessary. Again, "A value is a living and inexhaustible source of determinations" (Mounier 1952, 69).

Cultivating values, however, not only deepens one's sense of personal worth but unites a person to others. Value-formation, like personalization, "is constituted by a double movement . . . in fact, dialectical, on the one hand toward the affirmation of personal absolutes that resist any limitation, and on the other toward the creation of a universal union of the world of persons" (Mounier 1952, 29).[3] For the purpose of this study, such a compelling career objective suggests the need for a closer study of peoples' relations with each other.

Social Communion

Analysis of value espousals, and of the value-person above all, implies that people are related by more than external proximity but true interiority. This natural inclination to others inheres in the way people speak and think. The first person plural 'We' comes as naturally in discourse as the singular 'I.' The words people use to describe themselves are first applied to others. A person may style another as dull, mean, kind, just, or brave and perhaps characterize him or her as a lush, sharp financier, wise teacher, the soul of kindness, and so forth, but will tend to be more tentative in applying the same terms to oneself. Others—and especially enemies—see and judge one's failings more clearly than one can and does oneself!

Hence, to perceive others as manifesting the value-person is at the center of the human drama. To see beyond racial, gender, age, cultural, religious, political, and all the other ways people are differentiated to others' basic and equal dignity of personhood would ameliorate and go far toward resolving the conflicts that arise between and among people. Moreover, it accords with knowing oneself and others as more than naturally or fortuitously related but essentially social. Persons, even willful recluses, are enmeshed in a web of social ties and only know and evaluate themselves in light of their perceptions of their own or others' personalities and personhood. As such it becomes a life's career.

But nothing points up the deep need to see others as persons more than the tendency to form community. There may be many elements in the mutual male-female attraction—physical, moral, social, intellectual, economic, and so on—needed to create a family, but for true community spouses must see and respect each other and the children of their union as persons. Similarly, every kind of community—churches, schools, athletic teams, associations, enterprises, and the like—requires of all its members, besides sharing the value which differentiate the community, to accept every other member as a distinct and individual person. *True community is founded on the universality of the value-person.*

In sum, all natural tendencies to social communion require perceiving others as person. To do so is, consequently, both to discern an individual's highest quality and to demonstrate that oneself bears the value-person. Conversely, to know oneself as person creates the need to communicate that to others, as the baby needs to bond to a caring adult. "The person only exists . . . toward others, it only knows itself in knowing others, only finds itself in being known by them" (Mounier 1952, 20). In a sense a person sees self as existing as person only by grace of others. Reciprocally and in a real sense, a person can exist for others by giving oneself to others, by loving them.

All this implies seeing the other as a value, as a being, nature and quality perceivable as good. What draws one person to others is discerning their goodness and thus cultivating and espousing the values they manifest. This attraction in its most generous form is to bestow oneself without stint or hope of gain. Such openness to others implicitly recognizes—as opposed to an individualism which encloses a person in self—one's essential attachment to others. In this sense personalism argues for and stresses humanity's solidarity. But this unity is not of clones but of persons diversely individual and different yet all authentically members of the human race. The conviction that the human race is "one and indivisible is implicit in the modern notion of equality" (Mounier 1952, 29). In short, however lowly or degraded an individual, he or she is still a person.

Reciprocal to perceiving the other as person is to deepen one's own sense of personhood. "The person is only growing in so far as he is continually purifying himself from the individual within him. He cannot do this by force of self-attention, but . . . by making himself available and thereby more transparent both to himself and to others" (Mounier 1952, 19). This, in turn, demands a kind of internal conversion by way of changing one's values into real guides of one's thinking, acting, and conversing with others.

Such speculation may seem far removed from the nitty-gritty of production, trading, and investing. But not so, since the agents and subjects of economics are human persons, whose physical welfare is of concern to them just as is their spiritual well-being. This, then, requires viewing economic relations from a personalist point of view.

PERSONALIST ECONOMICS

While Mounier tends to the poetic, he sees personalism in a realistic way. For him it "is not a kind of spiritual doctrine, but rather the reverse. It includes every human problem in the entire range of concrete human life, from the lowliest material conditions to the highest spiritual possibilities" (Mounier 1952, 9). Dealing with the whole person, personalism has no less concern for peoples' material as for their spiritual realities.

This personalist course, therefore, acknowledges that every economic act involves in one way or another a quantitative ratio: so much given for so much gained. Thus, it accepts economics as an empirical and mathematical science addressing a unique aspect of human and natural reality with an entirely valid methodology. Nevertheless, it ascribes to Adam Smith's common sense criterion of what denotes an economy as both just and thriving:

> No society can . . . be flourishing and happy, of which the far greater part of the members are poor and miserable. It is but equity, besides, that they who feed, clothe, and lodge the whole body of the people, should have such a share of the produce of their labor as to be themselves tolerably well fed, clothed, and lodged (Smith 1937, 79).

The personalist view of the economy, therefore, as a human, but many-faceted and self-generating system, insists that a few primary principles, fashioned parallel to basic economic ideas and formulated to modify economic theories and conclusions, will make economic analysis both more humane and more realistic. The rest of this chapter, therefore, will examine from a personalist point of view three—of many—of the economy's basic principles. First is every person's *dependence* on material nature: as embodied spirits, humans need what nature provides in order to live and act. This dependence, in turn, requires that people *operate* in changing these same resources into useful products. Then, in a final and integrating phase, this output is *shared*

in accord with economic as well as personalist principles. Economic persons
are both economic doers and economic analyzers and as such dependent on
material nature.

Persons' Dependence on Nature

The personalist view of the human as *embodied self-awareness* underscores
the person's essential unity of matter and spirit. The fundamental personalist
principle here is the inherent link between people and the material world. Being biological, humans need air, water, food, clothes, shelter, and so on. As
mammals, they need mates and the means to support and protect their young
through infancy and puberty. Mobile, they need range, vehicles, and con-
veyances. As fabricators, persons need tools and ways to diagnose the elements of earth's resources.

Consequently, the affirmation that persons are body-spirits further stresses
their total reliance on physical nature. Not only are material things like food,
liquid, hide, structure, and fabric essential for survival, but a person's moods,
feelings, and spiritual states are shaped both by age and experience as well as
conditioned by geography, climate, physical circumstances, and associates.
An even more telling bond of matter to spirit is that the person's highest aspirations and most exalted sentiments must be expressed through material
means, from the most subtle, like color, sound, and electricity to the most
solid, like stone and steel.

Truly, men and women's most soaring flights of spirit entail mundane economics. Michelangelo's genius, for example, in drawing out of stone an all-
but-breathing figure of a handsome youth, bold, heroic, and tensed for com-
bat, required his buying a block of marble. Then, too, a patron's generosity
had to subsidize his vision and skill. While for centuries millions have stood
in awe before his *David*, yet it is owing to a benefactor's gain seeking and
the wage labor of a crew of stonecutters. In summary, men and women's
need for physical nature is total, ranging from the barest material to the most
sublimely spiritual.

Their dependence on the world of matter also extends vertically from what
they *need* for survival and careers to what they *want*, would like to have but
could forego. Needs are essential: what one cannot not have. They are mostly
stated as universals: food, shelter, travel. Wants make up the much larger category of desired specific things: a hamburger, that Cape Cod house, a BMW.
Such are nonessential, often substitutable one for another, or may be foregone
altogether. In short, the range of needs to wants extends from goods necessary
for survival, to what an important purpose requires, to things simply desired,
and on to trivial impulses of a fleeting fancy.

Compounding all this, needing and wanting are continuously changing, as human creativity and technology develop new ways of satisfying old desires. Culturally induced, these new products may become so widely wanted as to become quasi needs. Although basic needs for food, liquid, and shelter are as necessary now as in primitive societies, novelties and curiosities of an earlier period and culture can become almost required in a later society. In sum, person, as spirit/body, as needing or wanting, as culturally sophisticated or primitive, in a dynamic or a stagnant economy, is totally dependent on the physical universe.

Besides, this material universe is a fascinating environment, enchanting in its diversity, generous in its bounty, but awesome in its unpredictable destructiveness. Necessary for survival and growth in personhood, this physical world yet demands human care and management. "More and more clearly, science and reflection are confronting us with a world that cannot do without man, and with man who cannot do without the world" (Mounier 1952, 9). From the cave to now persons have seen the task of taming nature to human use as essential. Thus, even as they have been modifying nature, they have been modified by it. In sum, persons are bound to the material universe not just externally but internally: they are set in a dialectic of mutually creating products and desires.

This is simply to say that all material things, specifically all economic goods and services, are seen as bearing a value in the range from useful to useless to harmful. While that value-range implies a further value or values from sensual to sacred, economics as such treats only of the value-utility. (The further question how moral values relate to the value-utility is put off to chapter 6.)

In sum, all the linkage of human hopes, thoughts, and actions to the material world reaffirm that moral and humanistic answers to pragmatic issues must pass scientific and economic scrutiny to be useful and, conversely, the latter's solutions to problems must consider persons and moral aspects to be valid.

Thus, economics, as an empirical science, may concern itself solely with value-free wants and wanting insofar as these acts, by using material means, effect the demand for scarce goods and services. But even so, economists as well as every economic person must at least be aware that what people want and demand is subject to the higher criteria of what is needed and necessary and what values their needs and wants imply.

By increasing control over the forces of nature, which are as often cruel and heartless as they are nurturing and benign, the human race has gained a modicum of liberation from nature's most potent and most insidious powers and, even more so, has put many of these same forces to use for human betterment. In this sense, the further conclusion can be formulated that production

is an essential activity for persons. "Shackled at first to the immediate satisfaction of elementary needs . . . production should at last become . . . both lib-
erated and liberating, shaped by all the requirements of personality" (Mounier
1952, 14).

The Personalization of Production

While nature's palette of marvelous matter—living/lifeless, wild/tame,
field/forest, organic/inorganic, mineral/metal, solid/liquid, inert/vibrating,
and so on—provides an endless agenda for study and investigation, there is
little there for immediate human use. Almost everything has to be hunted, cul-
tivated, mined, fabricated, transmitted, analyzed, or otherwise changed to satisfy human needs and wants. Hence, the work of transforming nature's
bounty into something for human use becomes an obligation one way or other
for nearly everyone in the course of his or her life.

Human work, therefore, as an absolute necessity for serving people's ever-
renewing physical and spiritual needs and wants, becomes an obligation imposed on all—even teenagers!—except the totally incapacitated. Obliged to
work, persons have a right to work. This does not necessarily mean a job, being employed by another, and surely does not imply being forced to work beyond one's ability. But it does mean that people in general should contribute
to the economy's output in rough proportions to their sharing in it. (The obvious exceptions, children, the handicapped, the infirm, even shirkers, can
claim sustenance appropriate to their needs and status.) Moreover, whatever
an individual's work or however remunerated, work is a way of growing into
and expressing one's *personality*, of mastering and using *nature's powers*, of
caring for the *human habitat*, of maintaining the *common good,* and, all in all,
relating to and benefiting other people.

Thus basic to all production is the need to translate human needs into specific wants and the products to satisfy them. This, in turn, encourages producing not for personal use only but for other, even unknown, people. The
task, therefore, of working up matter to service personal needs and wants is
obviously a social activity on two counts: first, tasks are differentiated and
tend to be assigned as individuals' skills and interests suggest what is best for
production, and, second, what is socially produced should be socially shared.

Even in primitive cultures group activities like hunting or village moves
demand overall direction, organization, division of labor, and sharing. Personal handcrafting also requires some organization: locating materials and
fashioning them for use and for exchange within or beyond the tribe. Whether
all such production is governed by custom, by popular will, or by authority,
it requires some organization. All production, however rudimentary, therefore, necessitates *subordination* of some people to others.

Subordination, or course does not require subjugation. More frequently it means freely chosen subservient roles by which all who participate in the productive process share in its benefits. (True, Junior's leaf raking does exemplify inhuman subjugation!) In more complex economies, production is both affected and effected by cooperation among those who hire and those freely hired. Such interaction in production is not like that exacted from materials, machines, or animals, but it is a collaboration of human persons who join in production not only from necessity for livelihood but freely for personal gratification and even spiritual reasons. (The laborer in repairing a sewer not only performs a public good but may be manifesting love for his wife and children.) Producing socially is both more efficient and often preferred to working alone.

Work, for sure, is work. But despite its onerousness, its societal necessity involves elements of special importance for persons. First, working conditions should be such that dangers to health and safety are reduced to a minimum, clearly known and accepted by the workers and, if possible, compensated for. More importantly, organized work is social, entailing interacting with others. Such cooperation is further enhanced if charged by the belief that the product is what people want and is good for them. Lastly, the work climate must be geared to encourage—especially by rewarding—industry and efficiency. Obviously, therefore, work is an essential form of *economic praxis* and natural for the economic person.

The problem, however, for free enterprise and competitive production is profit-seeking capitalism. Efficiency here means using the minimum and least costly of labor, material, and energy to produce what people will buy. As such, it is the value which rules production for profit. But it is not absolute, as the mule skinner learned who worked his mule longer and longer days and fed it less and less until the beast up and died! That is, efficiency must encourage industry, the personal vital value central to work. As the zest for working diligently and well, the virtue of industry signifies an interest in the job and a response to its challenge. But it also requires being generally satisfied with compensation, working conditions, and the respect shown workers as persons.

Where these two values describe the work environment, shops, offices, and laboratories are on the way to a sense of community. But when profiteering dominates production, such deluded profit seeking inevitably generates what Marx calls "alienated labor:"

> Alienated labor had four aspects to it. First, the worker was related to the product of his labor as to an alien object. . . . Second, the worker becomes alienated from himself in the very act of production. . . . Third, man's "species-life," his social essence, was taken away from him in his work. . . . Fourth, man found himself alienated from other men (McLellan 1975, 31).

While Marx describes the pit into which industrial relations can descend, his paradigm of alienated labor as routinized work under sweatshop conditions pertained to a minority of workers in his own day and fell far short of predicting the labor scene in developed industrial economies today. Then, most workers by far were farm laborers, weavers, or village craftsmen. Now, economic growth and continuous product proliferation has diversified the work force and conditions beyond all imagining 150 years ago.

The vast changes in management, marketing, manufacturing, and household and technical maintenance; the constant diversification in personal, professional, public, and financial services; and the unprecedented development of research, travel, communication, and entertainment, all together, reveal an entirely different labor relations picture. First, it has broadened the concept of worker to include everyone from the night watchman to the president. It has also enlarged the corps of persons responsible for the goods and services produced to include many more than the capitalist stockholders. (Multiplication of stock ownership in fact dilutes most shareowners' responsibilities.) This huge army of workers, as a result, has left their imprints on products, some in hardly discernible ways, as goods flowed from idea to final sale, while others markedly influenced production as inventors, designers, and managers.

Finally, work is social in an organizational sense, as words like team, crew, cast, gang, staff, shop, office, comrade, mate, colleague, and partner imply, all of which suggest the natural tendency toward social and economic cooperation. All in all, while Marx's 'alienated labor' describes some jobs and is a valid warning as to what labor relations can become, it hardly describes the whole work scene of industrialized economies today. To the contrary, personalism presents production in a light more true to contemporary life.

It especially accents the most important principle relating to profit-seeking industrial cooperation, namely, that *labor has priority over capital*. Too often this is taken to mean that work for wages is more important than managing. Rather, it means that all persons involved, janitor to CEO, are workers, are those who make the enterprise go. Organization of the simplest company entails a complex of skills and functions: physical work, dexterity, and expertise, sales talent, analysis, and supervision and, above all, creative imagination and risk-taking. Thus, their remuneration should take precedence over that paid for inert, insensate productive means, materials, energy, machines, and money. Contra Marx and despite the inevitable selfishness, deceit, and injustice which intrude into all human actions, production is a totally and truly personalist process, which generates more goods than bads, at least in the sense of what people want. Work, therefore, is essential for the economy to function. Hence, it is both an honest and a necessary human activity, consistent with peoples' nature and serving to unite them as economic agents and persons.

Here morality and economics meet, since persons are simultaneously the most necessary productive factors as well as its agents, business is a human process and not just the mechanical workings of an anonymous organization. While business policies and performance may be unjust and greedy, economic acts are not alienated but the moral acts of persons, who are duty bound to respect and treat others justly and have destinies beyond the enterprise. Granted the difficulties in achieving this ideal, where managers strive for cooperative effort and honestly share the organization's gain business tends to go more smoothly and eventually to have more profits to share.

Sharing

Sharing completes the economic process: people's dependence on material nature, alleviated by social production, needs but sharing to humanize nature, to fulfill the preceding phases, and to bring the economic process full circle.

This sharing principle is well expressed in Smith's criterion that economies are functioning well, if those whose work yields the goods and services themselves get enough of the output to encourage their continued productive participation. Personalism adds two more principles, one positive and the other cautionary.

It is firm in insisting that, as there is a natural duty to humanize nature through social labor by fashioning the goods and services necessary for human survival and well-being, the general principle ruling economic production is that all share its output at least to a minimum subsistence level. That extends, for sure, to children, to the sick and infirm, and to all unable to support themselves. But it also includes those who from circumstances beyond their control or even by their own fault cannot provide adequately for themselves and their families. This principle, finally, also includes the obvious economic principle that those contributing to production be compensated roughly proportionate to the value of their contributions.

Personalism adds a cautionary precept: persons can have too much for their own moral good. Though needing goods and services to achieve one's vocation, career, and destiny as person, people can become enslaved by food, drink, drugs, clothes, and whatever. But sensuality can impair economic behavior as well as coarsen an individual's personal conduct. Alexis de Tocqueville shows the relationship in the reverse: The principle of self-interest "by itself cannot suffice to make a man virtuous, but it disciplines a number of persons in habits of regularity, temperance, moderation, foresight, and self-command" (Tocqueville 1966, 499). Wealth, initially possessed, may evoke a certain elation from the prestige riches bestow, but like energy, that glory is subject to entropy. Wealth is not an end in itself nor by itself freeing; possessions can splinter one's intentions and concerns and even enslave a person. At its worst, the desire to possess becomes a totally irrational passion to accumulate for its own sake. At best, it requires sharing with others.

Consumerism can also take the form of invidious consumption, the desire to have the very latest of everything, especially the most showy in order to garner others' envy. But the worst form of economic having is wealth-accumulation for the power it gives over others. Almost always that power, the power to purchase or money, is gained at the expense of others. Its gaining included an element of injustice. In summary, all forms of consumerism but especially the last two, intemperate and unjust gaining, both violate the inherent relation of persons to the material universe and block the social actions by which that relation is achieved.

Once again, therefore, moral and economic common sense meet. In every case unbridled seeing/wanting/having violates both the fundamental economic principle of diminishing marginal utility and the moral principles, that material goods must be shared and that consumption is not an end in itself. Controlling consumerism, in turn, confirms the suggestions made earlier that seeing men and women as persons not only reveals their basic human dignity and the significance of their lives and careers but strongly urges that a personalist perspective can modify economic concepts and qualify the application of economic principles.

In further conclusion, it is clear that persons as self-knowing, self-assessing creatures are free and responsible beings who are incarnated in matter and time. As such they know themselves best by knowing and evaluating other things and persons, thus achieving their destinies related to and in community with each other. Applying these realities to economic thinking reinforces the premise that human persons are necessarily social and at the same time inherently bound to nature and the material world. *They are economic persons.*

Therefore, as simultaneously an economic and a moral agent, the human person joins others in the work of humanizing nature for humankind's betterment with the necessary consequence that the benefit of that social task must also be shared with others. Thus one's career and destiny as person inescapably requires, as contributor, beneficiary, or both, sharing in the common economic enterprise. This consistence between economic and personalist premises yields the realistic hope for a more humanistic kind of economic science.

* * * * *

The remaining chapters will then describe how a personalist perspective modifies some basic economic concepts and principles to fit better the reality of the human person as a self-knowing, free, and responsible being and agent. Chapter 5 will review the problem of economic scarcity, that is, the constant struggle to make ends meet and the inevitability of prices as an essential condition of the person as an embodied spirit who needs material goods to survive. Chapter 6 demonstrates how economic values conform to one's value hierarchy and moral rules. Chapter 7 then analyzes gain seeking both as rational appetite and as the drive which makes the economy go. Chapter 8 examines how persons as simultaneously individual and social relate to each other in community and interact with moderation, justice, and generosity as moral beings. Chapter 9 shows how the three social values, Liberty, Equality, and Fraternity, interrelate in the Common Good and especially the economy's role therein. Last, Chapter 10 clarifies the concept of self-interest and the blending of economic contraries.

NOTES

1. Emmanuel Mounier (1905–50) is still an attractive source of personalist thought both for his penetrating insight and his felicitous phrasing. His *Personalism*, which came out the year before his death, can be assumed to summarize his conception of personalism. Nevertheless, it does not amount to a philosophical system nor even a fully fleshed treatise on personalism. Rather, it reflects his personal pilgrimage from his childhood's bourgeois Catholicism to the Christian mysticism of Leon Bloy, Charles Peguy, and Jacques Chevalier, then on to the neothomism of Jacques Maritain, even Marxism and Nietszchean existentialism, all the while remaining faithfully Catholic. Hellman concludes that Mounier elevated "a concern for the human person as the prime means of reforming Christianity" (Hellman 1981, 255). This conviction he blended into a career of social commentary and activism before, during, and after France's crucial war years.

2. The value ideas expressed here are mainly owing to the thought of Max Scheler, the German phenomenologist (1874–1928). They are further developed in chapter 6, "Personal and Economic Values."

3. How prophetic is this statement is easily demonstrated in that Charles Malik perceived in the concept of person the basis for the Universal Declaration of Human Rights. (Novak, Michael, "Human Dignity, Human Rights," *First Things*, Nov. 1999, 39–42)

REFERENCES

Amato, Joseph. *Mounier and Maritain: A French Catholic Understanding of the Modern World.* University: University of Alabama Press, 1995.

Danner, Peter L. *Getting and Spending: A Primer in Economic Morality.* Kansas City, Mo.: Sheed & Ward, 1994.

Evans, C. Stephen. *Preserving the Person: A Look at the Human Sciences.* Downers Grove, Ill.: InterVarsity Press, 1977.

Hellman, John. *Emmanuel Mounier and the New Catholic Left, 1930–1950.* Toronto, Ont.: University of Toronto Press, 1981.

Kavanaugh, John F., S.J. *Recovery of Personhood: An Ethics After Post-Modernism.* Milwaukee, Wis.: Center for Ethics Studies, Marquette University, 1994.

Marshall, Alfred. *Principles of Economics.* 9th ed. Edited by C. W. Guillebaud. London: Macmillan, 1961.

McLellan, David. *Karl Marx.* New York: Viking, 1975.

Mounier, Emmanuel. *Personalism.* Translated by Philip Mairet. South Bend, Ind.: University of Notre Dame Press, 1952.

Novak, Michael. "Human Dignity, Human Rights." *First Things* (November 1999): 39–42.

Scheler, Max. *Formalism in Ethics and No-formal Ethics of Value: A New Attempt toward the Foundation of an Ethical Personalism.* Translated by M. Frigs and R. Funk. Evanston, Ill.: Northwestern University Press, 1973.

Smith, Adam. *An Inquiry into the Nature and Causes of the Wealth of Nations.* Edited by E. Cannan. New York: The Modern Library, 1937.

Tocqueville, Alexis de. *Democracy in America.* Translated by George Lawrence and edited by J. P. Mayer and Max Lerner. New York: Harper & Row, 1966.

Chapter Five

Personalism and Scarcity

The personalist view of economic matters must, for certain, begin by perceiving the human person as embodied and necessarily dependent upon the universe of matter. But it is an inescapable fact of life that little from the material world is of use as is but must be explored, fabricated, and marketed to be serviceable. Economists call all such manufactured goods and services scarce, thus giving a peculiarly economic twist to the word "scarcity."

That economics' basic problem is even described as scarcity instead of by a more elegant Greek term like *catallactics* or *chrematistics* has had some consequence for the science's popular acceptance. Hardly a pleasing invitation to the study, implying as it does want, penury, and poverty, scarcity inevitably recalls Carlyle's name for economics, the "Dismal Science."

Even so, some economists in the desire to distinguish their science from other moral and social sciences will use terms with moral meaning carelessly, for instance, equating self-interest and selfishness. Others discard wholesale early economic thought with its religious, moral, political, and pragmatic bent in their emphasis on economics' scientific—that is, its mathematical and empirical—character. Again, some, by suggesting that economic criteria only apply to business matters, encourage businessmen and businesswomen along the paths of injustice and greed. All together these practices suggest to many people and even to scientists in related fields that economics treats of a dog-eat-dog struggle for survival instead of something natural to the human condition.

Ideas like these coalesce to raise the hackles of scholars in adjacent fields and suggest generally that economic scarcity arises from human iniquity. Two examples from random reading in other areas come to mind.

THE PROBLEM WITH SCARCITY

Psychologist Paul C. Vitz, in his *Psychology as Religion: The Cult of Self-Worship*, analyzes masterfully the contemporary cultivation of and pervasive stress on self, selfishness, and the unlimited gratification of wants as ultimate human values. As a consequence, he sees the cult of Selfism as a necessary support of industrial economies. He says, "Just as Western economies began to need consumers, there developed an ideology hostile to discipline, and to the delaying of gratification. Selfism's clear advocacy of experience now, and its rejection of inhibition or repression was a boon to the advertising industry" (Vitz 1994, 91). Obviously Vitz sees economic scarcity as owing mainly to self-indulgence rather than as inherent in the human condition.

On the other hand, theologian M. Douglas Meeks, in *God the Economist: The Doctrine of God and Political Economy*, defends God against the charge of stinginess in providing for His people, as he thinks scarcity implies. Like Vitz he concedes that excessive wanting contributes to scarcity but he instead blames capitalists and suppliers generally for artificially restricting supply:

> What the market mechanisms actually require is scarcity in the sense of withheld or locked access to what people need for livelihood and work. Scarcity in this sense is the condition for exclusive private property. But as justification for this, the meaning of scarcity is made to trade on the character of the human being as infinite desirer and infinite acquisitor. (I)n almost all situations of human life scarcity has been caused by human injustice. . . . For in general the biblical faith teaches that there is enough if the righteousness of God is present and acknowledged as the source of life (Meeks 1989,172, 174).

Thus, the latent difficulties laypeople have with scarcity, the trouble it regularly provides noneconomist scholars, and the problems it occasionally raises even for economists all urge a more lucid analysis, here for one, by examining in a personalist way peoples' fundamental dependence on matter. This dependence, moreover, is conditioned by the fact that at any moment there is never enough of most of what people need and want, so that they cannot have everything they fancy just for the taking. In short, this situation poses this question: why is it that almost everything people want must be paid for and is not free?

While Vitz and Meeks see economic scarcity as originating in disordered human conduct, insatiable appetites by one, and greedy market manipulations by the other, both would surely agree that sensuality, greed, and other vices are not unique to the economic factor in human conduct. They can and do disorder other human purposes, even those more sacred than the economic. Since such vices are not essential ingredients of economic relations and in no way necessary for life's daily business, they therefore cannot be defining features of economic actions. On the other hand, economists could assert more explicitly that the economic order would run more smoothly if people acted less selfishly and more justly in their business conduct. Economists would also help if they made greater efforts to interrelate their field with those of the moral sciences. Finally, moralists would be less wary of economics if its basic issue were more clearly identified as inherent to the economic person's physical nature.

All the above suggest that, as the result of the empirical revolution, scholars in different fields of inquiry, even those closely related, like the social and behavioral sciences, have trouble understanding each other. They illustrate the semantic problems that haunt interdisciplinary discourse and exemplify how human knowledge has become fragmented and compartmentalized. They witness to the loss of a synoptic view of the human experience, which Alisdair MacIntyre sees as a result of the knowledge revolution and industrial technology today:

> Ours was once a culture in which the systematic interrelationship of these questions was recognized by both philosophers at the level of theory and in the presuppositions of everyday practice. But once we left behind the ancient, medieval, and early modern worlds, we entered a culture largely and increasingly deprived of the whole. . . . Each part of our experience is detached from the rest in quite a new way; and the activities of intellectual inquiry have become divided and compartmentalized along with the rest. The intellectual division of labor allocates problems in a piecemeal and impartial way: and the consequent modes of thought answer very well to the experience of everyday life (MacIntyre 1979, 22).

The quote suggests also that disunity might arise from the differing ways scholars and scientists in the various fields of knowledge approach and know their subjects. A cursory review of these might help to clarify the point.

THE WAYS OF HUMAN KNOWING

Epistemology, the philosophy and science of truth and certitude in knowing, has been fought over for three millennia. Much of this is reflected in the current debate between devotees of the scientific empirical/inductive and those of the philosophic introspective/deductive method. The straightforward, pragmatic approach here, a kind of Aristotelian common sense, will proceed from the universal personalist experience, that what people see, feel, and so on really does exist, even though the knower may misinterpret what the senses present. *When persons know, they know something as something.* Even when not grasping the natures of the objects of their knowledge, people can still confidently date, count, weigh, and measure the things and persons that they encounter in life.

This conviction is the springboard for the vast increase in fact gathering and the inductive reasoning therefrom, called the scientific revolution. In scrutinizing every aspect of life, social relations, and material reality, this voracious appetite has explored the cosmos, mapped the globe, exploited the world's resources and potencies, uncovered human history, extended human life, and, sadly, developed horrible ways of destroying it. All aspects of physical reality, including human persons and their interrelationships, can be categorized, timed, aligned, trended, indexed, correlated, dissected, and otherwise processed in a vast arsenal of scientific scrutiny and analysis. While particular methods of collecting and interpreting data may be disputed, few doubt that the "real" is found in observed facts and events.

All considered, the inductive, scientific method with its process of empirical testing from hypothesis to theory to law is the marvel of the ages. Because of it, more than any other factor, Western civilization vaulted in five centuries from one of the more backward cultures to world dominance today. Science has given persons unprecedented knowledge of, and consequently control over, the forces of nature and has also given them wonderful understanding of their bodies, psyches, and social nature.

But scientific analysis cannot explain all of reality: correlation is not causation; probability is not essentiality; randomness is not freedom; sequence is not action. Nor can science, however well it documents human activity, capture the feelings, attitudes, and intentions which move persons to act. Finally and most importantly, it stops short of revealing what is the end and purpose of the cosmos and why people are in it. Answers to these must be sought in philosophy's method of deducing principles and applications from experiences, insights, visions, or revelations.

Deductive Philosophizing

Quite unlike the triumphant progress of scientific learning, the philosophic introspective/deductive method has produced more confusion than agreement. From the time when Descartes (1596–1650) drove a wedge between speculative and empirical reasoning, in effect defining humans as ghosts within machines, the philosophy of human understanding has veered between the extremes of La Mettrie's (1709–51) Materialism and Berkeley's (1685–1753) Idealism and since then into all the stops in between. More than once pronounced dying or dead, philosophy always revived as scholars returned to it to seek the meaning for living now and hereafter, of being, humanity, divinity, knowing, loving, truth, and right. Further, however confusing philosophic analysis may become, one can always return to the most basic and empirical knowledge of all, the fact of one's own existence. Socrates' counsel, *"Know thyself,"* not only is fundamental moral advice but is the basis for absolute certitude because to doubt it is to affirm it.

Consequently, however bewildering deductive philosophizing may become, a philosophy based on one's self-awareness insists on the empirical evidence of one's own being: knower and known being identical, no doubt is possible. To know at all is to know something or someone and in so doing implicitly to know oneself as knowing. Thus self-knowing and self-awareness implicitly occur simultaneously with knowing something else. Persons cannot know anything as fact if they are not at least implicitly aware of knowing that they know.

Furthermore, neither path to knowing can forego the other. The geneticist splicing DNA and the archeologist who has just found the shinbone of Hammurabi must, by the acts of announcing their findings, know that they are and who they are and that they fully realize what they are doing. Their self-awareness continues even in organizing their findings, correlating them to preceding facts, drawing further conclusions, and formulating other hypotheses. No less may philosophers, when meditating on the meaning of living and being, lose contact with physical and temporal reality or their relations with other people. In short, the collaboration of induction and deduction is as necessary for human learning as right-foot/left-foot alternation for walking.

Thus this simplified presentation can conclude with the conviction that both scientific and philosophic methods of seeking to know attest to peoples' commonsense, universal, and life-long experience that they are not locked into themselves but are open to and in contact with others and the universe. As an *embodied self-awareness*, a person can know not only the time and place of physical beings but their natures and reality. In sum, both ways of human knowing are mutually clarifying. The axiomatic *"I am,"* therefore, is the foundation of human certitude— the pivot upon which both introspective and empirical knowledge turn, relate to each other, and organize one's understanding, experience, and acts.

EXPERIENCE AND ACTION

The way humans perceive reality and act, therefore, mirrors their ways of knowing: the fragmentation of modern living—to recall MacIntyre— is reflected in today's piecemeal knowledge. Thus the simplest act can be dissected into many facets, any one of which may be, and often is, taken as its defining feature.

Indeed it is true that all physical reality is multifaceted and thus any human act can become the subject of many sciences and disciplines. Jane, for example, may ask Filmore to buy some bread on his way home from work. The act is obviously economic because economic values are exchanged. It illustrates marital harmony also, relating to an important social event, the family meal. Being the transfer of private property, it concerns civil authorities. As nutritional, it interests health-care providers. Biologists and chemists have a say, because it relates to vital and elemental reality. Physicists may examine the bread's path to market through space and over time and chart Filmore's route home. Overall, moralists may question whether justice and love permeate and motivate the act. Thus the simplest act can ramify through all fields of inquiry, every branch of knowledge having its say, regardless what others present.

Further, empiricism's inherent logic requires following the facts wherever they lead. Consequently, conclusions arising in one field of inquiry may impinge on those in another. Absent clear principles, which distinguish the specific view of reality relevant to each science, the understanding of even the simplest act, event, or thing is fraught with confusion. Also the findings of one science must be carefully phrased so as not to impugn conclusions of another. (For example, contrary to what people often say, prices are never unjust. The person exacting the price may be acting unjustly but a price is right if it does what a price should do, effect an exchange, and is wrong if it does not.) In sum, much controversy will be obviated by clearer understanding and expressing the exact scope of inquiry and the basic problems that each science addresses. Such care will not only preserve each science's distinctness but will demonstrate how insights from one field may enrich those from another.

Again, a personalist approach can suggest how the sciences interrelate. A personalist philosophy, to recall Mounier, is not just a spiritual doctrine, but "includes every human problem in the entire range of concrete human life, from the lowliest material conditions to the highest spiritual possibilities" (Mounier 1952, 9). A personalist view of reality not only links introspective and empirical knowledge but sets a reference point for every science. While it may be true that most scientists pursue research simply for the satisfaction of knowing, once their findings enter the public domain, others will see how the knowledge can be used to understand human beings better and to further their well-being. Thus personalism by linking the ways of knowing also provides a focus in the nature of persons to which all sciences can relate.

Person as Focal Point

Thus persons as self-knowing and self-judging are first and preeminently moral beings called to relate to others and marked for a final destiny. As creatures who know themselves best in knowing and relating to things, animals, and especially to other persons, they consummate careers as social beings by emulating the civic, cultural, personal, and moral values others manifest in their lives and actions and by avoiding their vices. Inhabiting the universe and this earth, persons are very much concerned to know whatever they can of the physical, chemical, and biological forces which rule here and throughout the cosmos. Indeed, human life today would be difficult without the health, psychological, and social sciences professions. Last, individuated and embodied spirits need physical things to survive, to learn, to relate to others, and to express themselves. In sum, personalism provides a focal point toward which all lines of human knowledge converge. It offers, therefore, a means for resolving conflicts between and among the sciences and provides a way to repair the fragmentation of human experience and human knowledge.

As such, the preceding leads to the thesis of this chapter. To understand economics as the science of satisfying human needs and wants by way of cooperative production and sharing requires perceiving all economic agents as persons. It implies, also, the concurrent proposition that, contrary to critics like Vitz and Meeks, economic 'scarcity' is no more due to human iniquity than other human problems but is rooted in human personhood. On the other hand, it concedes that economists may rub social and moral scientists the wrong way because of a kind of hubris in giving meanings to words which vary considerably from ordinary parlance.

For many critics of contemporary economics their dissension is accentuated because they were introduced to the prescientific but humanistic economics, detailed earlier, which treated economics from moral, practical, and legal viewpoints. The indifference with which many dismiss that approach today seems to be justified by the enormously successful role an empirical, quantitative, and almost mechanistic behavior of *homo economicus* is dominant in today's complex national and international markets and economies. In researching wherever the data leads, however, economic empiricism may heedlessly root into areas and proffer dicta about morals, ethics, laws, legislation, and personal relationships beyond its competence.

All these perils and pitfalls aside, the basic fact remains that economic agents, whether consumer, worker, or entrepreneur, are persons. Consequently, blending the quantitative/empirical and the philosophic/personal, while more complicated, will yield conclusions which are both more vital and more clear. It applies particularly to the concept of 'scarcity' which will be analyzed from both the empirical and introspective points of view.

SCIENCE AND ECONOMICS OF ABUNDANCE

Nothing belies the conception of economics as the science of scarcity than the history of economics. Economics, as a matter of fact, achieved status as a science separate and distinct from moral philosophy during the empiricist revolution of the last 250 years, precisely the period when living conditions of Western nations and peoples improved more than during the previous 2,500. Despite all the suffering this abundance revolution entailed, it is as far off the mark to call economics the science of scarcity as to call agrobiology the science of barrenness. If anything, economics should be called the *science of abundance*.

Even more convincing is simply contrasting Cro-Magnon's life with that of people today. No data on farming, commerce, or production is needed to conclude that life then was hard and brief. Although inhabiting this same earth, as richly endowed with all kinds of energy—solar, wind, water, heat, electric, bacterial, nuclear, electromagnetic, and more—and blessed as copiously with ores, minerals, stones, fuels, fabrics, and skins as people are today, they had little more than bare necessities. Further, it required millennia of thought, effort, failures, and dangers for humans to achieve the level of living China achieved by 1000 and Western Europe by 1750. But since then economic production has grown at average yearly rates inconceivable before.

But the real measures of economic betterment, the idealistic romanticizing of simpler living not withstanding, are changes in life expectancy, health care, nourishment, work, shelter, travel, recreation, and communication. Months of travel time are cut to hours and intercontinental communication to minutes. Work days from dawn to dusk are relieved by days and weeks of leisure and youth-to-death labor by years of retirement. The hovels the poor inhabited then are now commodious dwellings with air conditioning, plumbing, central heat, and television. Nourished by a steady flow and greater variety of foods and benefitting from modern medical marvels, babies' survival rates have increased dramatically and general life expectancies have doubled. Such facts, more so than engineering and productivity feats, give the real picture of the revolution in material living since 1750.

(This does not deny that affluent economies have destitute people, some from causes beyond their control and others because of vices and acts of their own responsibility. Indeed poverty is statistically necessary, when household incomes are ranked by deciles, quartiles, and medians, unless absolute income equality is mandated. That is, poverty is inevitable, even though it is far from destitution and, in itself, neither reason for shame or alarm. Distinguishing, therefore, between poverty and destitution requires different policies and actions in response to each.)

Therefore, however one views economic well-being, two factors among many others are basic contributing factors: the formalizations of empirical research and of the economic process.

Recorded empirical observations go back to Aristotle and perhaps earlier, but controlled experiments were rare even during the Renaissance. Up to

1750 science scholars were spread thinly across the world; amateurs mainly seeking to learn for the love of knowing. By contrast, scientists today are professionals who make their living by research. They are, says Teilhard de Chardin, "no longer . . . sporadically distributed across the human mass" but "functionally linked together in a vast organic system that will remain indispensable to the life of community" (Teilhard 1966, 106). This rising stream of knowledge of the cosmos, of earth's powers and potencies, and of humanity's nature and history is, of course, basic to continuously changing life on planet Earth. But that does not occur automatically; it still needs the economic process to translate this knowledge into more useful goods and services.

Empiricism and Economic Abundance

Economics, therefore, from the start of its scientific mode dealt with the facts of increasing wealth and well-being that, initially limited to the rich, were gradually shared by all, even the poorest. Great fortunes were created and often wrung from real wage slavery. But a freely growing economy, driven by the ambitious and risk takers and not just catering to complacent wealth, tends to spread abundance, because increased output will lower product prices and increased demand for labor raise wages. No other way explains how the general public came to realize the material plenty described above. Thus, while empirical sciences discover the earth's treasures, the economic process both rewards their finds and translates them into useful goods and services.

Thus the process is best seen as a continuous stream of acts of buying and selling, each minutely modifying and being modified by the flow. A blend of varied actions, it generates four distinct economic phases: innovating, investing, producing, and marketing, each requiring particular personal qualities. Innovating is the creative imagination intuiting ways to satisfy new wants and to transform or modify current production. Investing is risk taking: lending money or property, giving time or work, and gathering the resources needed to translate the idea into an economic product by which to recoup the original outlay plus a premium. That, in turn, requires organizing the human collaborators, resources, and equipment into a functioning team, producing, finally, what the marketers can persuade customers to want and buy. No enterprise, of course, is so neatly organized: the phases often blend into each other and require constant trial and error adjustments.

Finally, just as scholars and scientists work for pay, so too do all others who are engaged in economic activity. All want to better their temporal welfare, *to gain*. Innovators and inventors hope for large payoffs; investors hope for capital gains; producers and marketers need profits to keep going; and employees want salaries and wages to continue work. Consumers, too, hope to gain, expecting to be satisfied with what they buy for the prices they pay. It also suffices to point out that gain seeking is universal, applying to sports, the arts, churches, charities, government bureaus, and the like and that in all cases it is best contained by the threat and reality of competition. (All of this will be more fully discussed in chapter 8.) In short, while Meeks is right in insisting that earth is plentifully supplied with resources and energy, history reveals that they become available for human use only because of a vast, complex, and fascinating system of mutual, but self-interested, effort.

Thus, analysis so far yields the conclusion that persons are the obvious and necessary agents of both empirical research and the economic process. Next is to examine the person's role on the demand side of the economic process and, in so doing, to help clarify the problem of scarcity as really the problem of pricing.

PERSONALISM AND PRICING

However mechanistically the economy is perceived, no one can deny that persons as regulators, investors, inventors, workers, entrepreneurs, and consumers make the economy go. It is quite to the mark, therefore, to see personalism applying to the economic problem. While all facets of personhood, as social, moral, and value-espousing, have economic relevance, the person as embodied spirit is of immediate concern. For sure, persons can in thought, desire, memory, and imagination roam beyond the here and now and as social beings can by love become one with another. But as embodied, they are totally dependent for survival on food, drink, shelter, clothing, and health care and for sociability on sex, play, and public order. Then, too, persons know others and the world only by sensing colors, odors, sounds, flavors, and textures. Hence, persons as *embodied* spirits are absolutely and essentially involved in the economic order and everyone must take some part in the economic process. They are economic persons.

Their part, of course, impacts adversely when people pervert their needs and wants. Addiction to things harmful to health, and indulgent use of otherwise good products also stir markets in the wrong way. Also, impulses to gratify every whim and desire, what Vitz condemns as Selfism, surely have like effect. Indeed, all are a form of the very modern vice of Consumerism: the need and impulse to have more simply because more can be had, because others have more, or because having more is sign and evidence of importance. So, all told, human failings and vices can increase demand and raise prices, making others' buying more costly. But a more potent force than physical wanting is at work, one which arises from the person's nature as self-knowing but embodied spirit.

That is, economic persons require not only things to satisfy material needs but goods and services to gratify material and spiritual wants. Further, not only are the things by which people relieve their ever renewable wants, constantly changing, but the manner and mode of their satisfying are continuously being embellished or refined. Cuisine at ordinary dinners becomes as important as nourishment; style and fads as comfort and warmth; pleasure and romance as progeny; the body beautiful as health. Also once people begin to look beyond the tribe or village, ever newer and more convenient methods of travel and communication become musts. More involved play generates more polished entertainment, and more complicated ownership, housing, and traffic, a more intrusive government. All such creative ideas beget new businesses, usually requiring new technology, more refined skills and more extensive trade, all contributing to make the economic process more complex.

Matter and the Creative Spirit

But the person's creative spirit goes beyond merely refining physical needs to satisfying an array of cultural and emotional and especially spiritual needs—to know, to love, to feel, and to experience beauty—all of which have a material base. From the beginning, humans have worked up stone, glass, clay, pigment, bone, wood, metal, shell, fabric, and even trash into symbols of human beauty, family love, religious feeling, patriotism, and awe of nature. Fire and light are particular favorites to evoke the most soul-searing emotions. But sounds above all else have been converted into something as nearly spiritual as anything physical can be.

Sounds, of course, are simply vibrations in the atmosphere engulfing Earth. People share sound with animals like the howl milord emits when hammering the wrong nail or milady's shriek on winning top prize at bingo. But humans have developed sounds in more formal and organized ways in music and the spoken word. The human repertoire of meaningful spoken sounds undoubtedly grew over thousands of years, becoming ever more ruled, formalized, and particularized to specific groups of people. As such it was the principal way tribal wisdom, traditions, and stories were passed from one generation to the next until spoken sounds began to be translated into written symbols. Thereby speech lost something of its importance to writing but with radio, TV, theater, school, church, meetings, and daily conversation it is still one of the greatest intellectual and emotional forces in contemporary life.

Of greater magic are the ordered and patterned sounds called music. From a few standard notes, obtained by vibrating strings, blowing through pipes, beating metal, wood, hide or whatever, and especially from human voices—choral, group or solo—sounds are produced which evoke joy, sorrow, anger, love, patriotic fervor, religious feeling, and indeed the whole range of human moods and emotions. It has enlivened family circles, suffused cathedrals, aroused athletic teams, and marched men to battle. Music is the classic example of spirit quickening and energizing the potency of matter.

In a very real sense persons as embodied spirits use matter, which binds them to time and space, in the personal adventure to discover self, others, and all reality. In so doing they can roam the past or dream of the future, escaping in thought, intention, desire, or imagination both place and time, even this life itself. Furthermore, such wanting can aspire to the heights of human love and religious aspirations and yet descend into gross sensuality, viciousness, and hate. These yearnings of spirit, both noble and evil, drive persons' endeavors both to understand their humanity and this planet they inhabit and to bestow beauty, dignity, and meaning on structures, stones, sounds, and words. In the process matter is transformed into something akin to spirit and material wanting is etherealized so to express both the most exalted ideas and feelings and the worst intentions. All such efforts of spirit to transcend fixity in space and time underscores that persons can and do seek spiritual ends by using physical things.

Ironically, this very effort to transcend the material has created great industries, requiring high labor skills, enormous investments, and ever developing technology. It has generated a vast educational program, serving untold millions, a flood of books, plays, musical compositions, and architectural temples both to commerce and divinity. Finally, social impulses like friendship, compassion, and understanding and the opposites, envy, enmity, and indifference motivate much buying and selling. Life goals, such as struggles for power, popularity, and prestige, and the intense desires for truth, meaning, beauty, and good are powerful spiritual motives that affect mightily what is produced, traded, and consumed. All told, what drives the economy is the spirit's constant search for more, whether to fulfill its own aspirations or to indulge the body's urges. Mounier again comments cogently, "It is just not possible to be without having, true though it is, that personal being is an infinite capacity of having, that it is never fulfilled in whatsoever it may have, and that its meaning transcends all having" (Mounier 1952, 39).

Thus, just as persons' labor, ingenuity, and creativity are needed to transform the cosmos' powers and resources into useful products, so too persons' drives and dreams form an ever-increasing and ever-changing kaleidoscope of wanting. In this sense personalism sheds needed light on both supply and demand aspects of the economic problem.

Personalism and the Economic Problem

The fundamental economic problem, therefore, arises in part from the universal human experience that nothing persons have of material or spiritual goods is ever fully satisfying. Even so, in servicing material needs proper to material beings, a person's spiritual drive goes beyond physical satisfaction to seek goals which transcend them. On the other hand, this planet offers little of use just for the taking: more and more, people must organize their varied abilities and resources into a huge social liturgy to research, fund, and produce the goods and services people need and want. The personalist perspective, therefore, in perceiving humans as embodied spirits, whose soaring thoughts, hopes, ambitions, and social needs can be served only by limited material means, which they themselves must fabricate, finds the economic problem rooted in persons' nature and being. In short, persons as embodied spirits are both cause and solution of the economic problem.

A universal exchange process is mandated because persons, as wanting and providing economic goods, are both beneficiaries and producers. It is just as true for individuals—wanting a fire, a person must gather firewood—as for a whole population. One can get what others produce by producing what others want. Seen globally, therefore, the economic process is but an enormously complex exchange process in which wanting drives production. The economic problem, therefore, is the *problem of exchange* and once money, as means of exchange, is used universally, it becomes the *problem of pricing*.

Prices get to the real point of human experience. People in modern industrial economies, who might daily or weekly shop at a supermarket or visit a shopping mall, probably seldom experience scarcity in its ordinary meaning but they do experience prices. These are everywhere, under all circumstances and for every kind of commodity and service. Goods for sale may be rare or abundant but still priced. Jobs may be plentiful or few but in both cases command wages. Money, whether copious or in short supply, will bear interest. Salaries, dividends, royalties, and rents are prices; as are taxes, tolls, fines, and duties; admissions, bets, fares, tips, allowances, tuitions, and contributions. The universal experience of prices yields the certain conclusion that without a price system modern economies could not function: workers would not work, businesses would not produce, families could not buy, and governments could not govern. But, however necessary, prices still present problems.

They do, for sure, carry a whiff of scarcity. Prices mean that something must be surrendered (usually money) to get what is wanted, because unlike free things, more priced goods are wanted than are available. This hangover carries into the real difficulty with prices: the problem of making ends meet. That this tendency of spending prices to exceed income prices is clearly a problem relating more to abundance than to scarcity is exemplified best by the United States's government. Despite enjoying the largest income in world history, its annual spending more frequently exceeds its income. In so doing the United States is not unique among all the nations, businesses, and households in the world. Its tendency toward deficit spending is only the grossest.

So the problem of scarcity, in evolving into the problem of making ends meet, now raises questions about prices, what they do and how they arise, change, and relate to each other. Indeed, economic analysis demonstrates that any specific price is part of an infinite chain and vast network of prices, stretching back and forward in time and extending across the exchange universe. For these reasons economists gather libraries of data, fashion indices, and work out correlations to explain all the conditions and the factors—every birth and death, every change in wants and tastes, every new technique and technology, every law, regulation, and statute—which change the prices of products, labor, and money.

Economists are justly proud and rightfully honored for this marvelous and complex set of laws, rules, and principles by which prices guide the where, when, and how human effort and the cosmos' resources and powers are used and intended in some way to better people's physical living. Economic science and the practical disciplines of management, marketing, advertising, finance, and accounting, plus the technologies spawned by the natural sciences have started a process that, for good or ill, will transform how all tribes and nations of Earthlings will live.

The Economy and Human Solidarity

Ironically, it is this very triumphalism which makes other scholars, especially in the moral disciplines, uneasy. Does the universal human problem of making ends meet mean that the economy is some kind of mindless robot, spewing out endlessly things of ever-diminishing value, a machine which only the unscrupulous can control and use to their sole benefit? Or is the economy really and generally beneficial to all men and women and the problem of making ends meet rooted in the human condition? These questions can be best answered by philosophic analysis and especially from a personalist perspective.

From this point of view it is apparent that this Earth could never have immediately available the smallest part of the vast amount and variety of material goods and services which people could want and have access to in the modern industrial economy. It is ludicrous to imagine otherwise. But from the personalist point of view the result is even more marvelous.

Seen from this perspective the human spirit has created over thousands of years, from the yet unmeasured resources and powers of the universe, a vast engine of production, serviced by billions of workers, managers, researchers, investors, financiers, regulators, and others, who provide the ideas, monies, techniques, and efforts by which people get the products and services they need and want. This comes to a worldwide on-time inventory problem, prices signaling what people want, what to produce, where to ship them, and what price to charge. Such becomes a system beyond the conception or intention of anyone or a committee of the world's brightest rulers, scholars, and industrialists. Rather, it evolved through the ages from tribal hunts to transnational corporations.

So scarcity or, better, making ends meet, is far from an expression of the stinginess of nature or of a supreme being, nor is it just a manifestation of human perversity, sensuality run amuck, or greed taking advantage of others. A personalist view, while conceding the susceptibility of human endeavors to intemperance, injustice, and all the vices, nevertheless detects the cooperative lineaments of all economic systems from the most primitive to the most complex. All respond to conditions shared by all human persons, individually and collectively, that their wants and hopes transcend their material means. The problem of making ends meet, of wants pushing beyond the means to have, is embedded in the human person and basic to the human condition. It in turn suggests the questions of what is worth seeking and what *values*, moral and/or economic, should guide this quest.

REFERENCES

Danner, Peter L. "Personalism and the Problem of Scarcity." *Forum for Social Economics* 25, no. 1 (fall 1995).

MacIntyre, Alisdair. "The Frustrating Search for the Foundations of Ethics." The Hasting Center Report, 9 August, 1979.

Meeks, M. Douglas. *God The Economist: The Doctrine of God and Political Economy*. Minneapolis, Minn.: Fortress, 1989.

Mounier, Emmanuel. *Personalism*. Translated by Phillip Mairet. South Bend, Ind.: University of Notre Dame Press, 1952.

Teilhard de Chardin, Pierre. *Man's Place in Nature*. Translated by R. Hague. New York: Harper & Row, 1966.

Vitz, Paul C. *Psychology as Religion: The Cult of Self-Worship*. 2d ed. Grand Rapids, Mich.: William B. Eerdmans, 1994.

Wolf, A. *A History of Science Technology & Philosophy in the Eighteenth Century*. Revised by D. McKie. New York: Harper Brothers, 1952.

Chapter Six

Personal and Economic Values

As one's body grows and changes, so one's personhood changes and matures. Both changing patterns reflect and are reflected in the values persons espouse. Personalism presents this dynamic as a living activity of self-creation, which Kavanaugh calls an "embodied self-conscious drama," opening and developing through time and space (Kavanaugh 1994, 14). The person's interior richness is endowed not only with a continuity from repetition but with a transcendence, just as an airplane to stay aloft must point its nose upward (Mounier 1952, 67–8). Hence, persons can be regarded as striving for a transpersonality, which is revealed in a sense of community with others and especially in attaining "an *interior stronghold of values*, against which we do not believe the fear of death itself could prevail" (Emphasis added) (Mounier 1952, 70–1).

Values, therefore, not only bind one person to others but in this and in all ways values are "living and inexhaustible source(s) of determinations, an exuberance and radio-activity of ideas" (Mounier 1952, 69). This says that one's value system is a dynamic, whose constituent values are not always consistent but are changing and need frequent reformulation. It also means that values are not just nostrums for moral crises but insights into the meaning of the basest matter as well as infinite being. Thus, for people as economic agents, values are conditioned by how they function in the economy's production and by how they participate, as exchange values, in the economy's beneficence. As such, therefore, values pose some problems for economic thought.

Values, their lack or the wrong kind, are matters of general concern today. As contemporary mantras, they usually evoke more sentiment than sense. Words like *value,* meaning an imputed excellence, *worth*, an intrinsic excellence, and *good*, a thing sufficient for some purpose, are so near in purport as to be almost equivalent. Such resemblances complicate defining the differing ways values express a being's innate worth, the good imputed to it, or its utility or purchasing power. More to the point here, is the problem how personal, cultural, social, and moral values are related to and defined by economic and exchange values; that is, the prices of things and services needed to realize values in the first place. Thus values present two problems: (1) the need to sort out value priorities, those innate to human persons and those espoused in life's course and (2) to clear up the problems of relating those personal values to exchange values or prices.

PERSONALISM AND HUMAN VALUES

However varied their use, values still elicit some sense of the moral high road. Their real purpose and intention pertain to one's roles as citizen, as social, as moral being, as knowledge seeker, pleasure lover, and so forth—all values that constitute the life dramas of human persons. Indeed, the story of humanity says more about life's important purposes transcending the merely vital, sensual, and pleasurable. A person's history is more about striving for the hard to obtain than about compliance with what is already had.

The Human Ascent and Values

A sweep through human history from the presapiens toolmaker to the hunter/gatherer and on to the farmer, artisan, and trader, while primitive totemism and animism grew into a belief in some supreme powers or power, gives substance to such visions as that of the Jesuit geologist and philosopher, Teilhard de Chardin. He conceives a universal cosmogenesis, the world coming into being over eons as the life forces of the biosphere work on the basic matter of the geosphere, culminating in the noosphere, the human person. Thus all things, material, animal, and human converge in Omega, the Supreme Act of Love. Whether vision or myth, it is a powerful portrayal of homo sapiens' purposeful ascent from the cave (Teilhard 1960 and 1965).

This ascent affirms in a more personalist way the concept, pioneered by the Swedish psychologist Eduard Spranger, of character evolution as organic growth. Like a tree growing from seed, the person transcends its embryo though contained by it, conditioned by environment while transforming it, its growth systematic yet complex. Spranger sees the ego as a congery of many drives, biological, social, political, economic, aesthetic, intellectual, affective, and religious. An organism, struggling to survive, it must satisfy its physical needs. At the same time, it desires and wants to create beauty and seeks meaning in all things, in particular reaching out to other human beings, at times lovingly perceptive of their good and at other times imposing its will on them. All told Spranger represents personal growth as expanding outward as well as thrusting upward, while still rooted in its most elemental needs (Spranger 1929, 88–106). That anticipates this chapter's story.

Values display the same dynamics in being central to ethical theory and like the most profound aspects of personhood, can be approached from any side and many angles. Rescher assigns them both critical and teleologic roles, as norms for judging things' goodness and as reasons or goals for overt action (Rescher 1960, 2–3). Angell emphasizes their social significance by seeing them "as continuing qualities we desire to see realized" (Angell 1965, 18). Scruton distinguishes values from preferences and stresses their significance and authority in practical reason. People defend their values but not their preferences, because they "learn to see and understand the world in terms of them. A value is characterized not by its strength but by its depth, by the extent it brings order to experience" (Scruton 1979, 32). Allport then locates a value deep in the personality "as a belief upon which man acts by preference." It is "a deeply propriate disposition," which reveals a person's intentionality or central theme of his or her striving, that is, one's innate values (Allport 1965, 126–7 and 454).

A THEORY OF NATURAL VALUES

Finnis, on the other hand, bases his value theory on the personalistic principle of "experiencing one's nature . . . from the inside, in the form of one's inclinations" (Finnis 1980, 34). Thus, values are basic aspects of one's being. They are indemonstrable because *self-evident*. For example: "The principle that truth is worth pursuing is thus an underived principle. Neither its intelligibility nor its force rests on any further principle" (Finnis 1980, 69).

Finnis then defines seven innate aspects of the human person as basic values. Since he grants that others may define and array them differently, they are listed here with some variations and arranged differently. The most fundamental is the *value-life* and the values of health, nutrition, sanity, and safety it implies. For many it may encompass procreating and nurturing children. The *value-play* is a basic desire to have and to do things for the fun of it and to mingle caprice, wit, and humor into even the most serious enterprise.

The three spiritual drives, to know, to cultivate beauty, and to relate to other people in friendship and love, are at the very center of personal wanting. The *value-knowledge*, an eagerness to know, ranges from tavern gossip to scientific research. The *value-beauty* involves seeking aesthetic responses in whatever milieu and in creating beauty in whatever median. The *value-friendship* ranges from marital love to ordinary civility, all the ties which unite persons individually or socially. These three values are clearly interrelated and relate to the previous two. For example, the subset, *value-married-love*, joined to that of having and raising children, which is a subset of *value-friendship* and *value-life*, constitutes the distinct subset, *value-family* (Finnis 1980, 59–99).

The *value-religion* is experienced by everyone at some time or other about one's own and the cosmos' origin and their ultimate ends and purposes. For some their convictions about this become a ruling principle. But for most the daily decisions to do or not to do, to prefer this or that and so on, the *value-practical reasonableness* is all important. "It is the basic good of being able to bring one's own intelligence to bear effectively . . . on the problems of choosing one's actions and life-style and shaping one's own character" (Finnis 1980, 88). This value functions both about how to do or to make something but even more about how to exercise moral freedom.

More to the problem of the chapter, each or several of these basic values can become dominant by way of directing a person's economic calling, as, for examples, practical reasonableness to engage in business, curiosity-to-know to do research, aesthetic sensitivity to do or to enjoy the arts, a playful spirit to engage in sports, health concerns to practice medicine, marital love to beget and care for one's family, and so forth. "Each of us has a subjective order of priority among the basic values; this ranking is no doubt partly shifting and partly stable, but it is in any case essential if we are to act at all to some purpose" (Finnis 1980, 93–4). Here is where basic and economic values can and often do conflict, where persons' economic or social rewards do not match their dominant basic value or values. Resolving that problem, however, must wait on further analysis of the complementary problem of how persons espouse values empirically and from that form value hierarchies.

VALUES AND VALUE HIERARCHIES

Thus the study shifts its focus from the theory of innate value of Finnis's natural law philosophy to a theory of value formation by the phenomenologist, Max Scheler (Scheler 1973, 99–110). It will in this way both illuminate the *value-person* and demonstrate the drama of value formation as persons shape and reshape from daily experiences their hierarchies of dormant-to-dominant values.

The Value Experience

While few people can list the values they espouse or distinguish them from innate inclinations to the good, yet all functional values are acquired through life's experiences. Rarely would these be as dramatic as the Pharisee Saul's value experience on the road to Damascus. Most values begin with parent and teacher admonitions, start by self-criticism, or are triggered by experiencing a remarkable event or person. Again, one may simply realize that, after seeing Aunt Em's gentle and generous solicitude for others, she personifies the *value-kindness*. This is not to say she is the value: Em may pass on but the value remains as a measure for ranking other acts of kindness, including one's own. Values, therefore, cannot be defined but only described, and value experiences say more about the depth and clarity of the valuers' perception than about the objects so perceived and ranked.

Indeed, values add no more information about the object. To see another as kind is simply seeing him or her in a new light. In fact, values are perceived without knowing everything about an object, even all that might pertain to the value. Thus, valuing is like sensation, an act of immediate cognition, that is, without conceptualization. Unlike sensing, however, it intuits the goodness of objects, not their physical qualities. Hence also the will prefers the object as good. What is perceived as good is willed, and what is willed as good is valued. The value experience, therefore, is a complete act, simultaneously of both intellect and will of the human person. In short, values are realized *experientially*, *perceptually,* and *preferentially*.

As such, values impose an obligation to pursue the good which it manifests. This 'ought,' however, does not flow from a Kantian innate sense of duty. Rather, what should be sought is what is perceived as good. Nor are values determined by previous acts of the will but, rather, newly determine the will. Hence the value-experience precedes purpose, because a purpose is good or bad and must be pursued or avoided, depending upon whether the goal proposed bears a higher or lower value. Given innate inclinations to the good, values are still the subjective products of acts by the value-espouser. They are objective only in the sense of being derived from qualities of real objects. Two persons who honor the same flag share like but individual patriotic feelings. Both value-experiences, while equally powerful, will be differently motivating. In sum, values are intuitions into the goodness of persons, things, or of relations between and among people or things to people, which at the same time evoke preferences, or the placing of them in rank order with other values.

Since every person and thing is in essence good and good for something or someone, everything potentially manifests a value. Persons, individually or in a group or class, bear values. Human acts, whether spiritual, vital, sensual, unconscious responses, or instinctive reactions can be valued. A person's moral tenor may be valued differently than individual acts, intentions differently than feelings. Personal relations like marriage can be evaluated as such or in their present state. Things, too, bear values, being differentiated as spiritual, cultural, sensual, useful, and so on. Finally, values, like persons or art, are good in themselves, while tools, techniques, symbols, etc., are *means-values*. In sum, values differ according *to whom*, *in the way*, and *how* they are valuable, i.e., by preserving health, enlightening the mind, moving the will, or ennobling the heart (Rescher 1960, 13–9).

Thus values can brush against one at every turn of life and whisper at every level of being and personality. All of life, viewed horizontally or vertically, is potentially value-laden. Granted that most preferences are instinctive, reflexive, or even habitual, nevertheless, people evaluate persons, things, and their interrelations every day, judging them pleasant or unpleasant, helpful or harmful, beautiful or ugly, good or bad, holy or evil. While values, like air, totally envelop persons, they require some conscious effort to perceive them as such. For persons' moral as well as their economic lives the pragmatic effort to structure and form their value hierarchies is, therefore, most important.

Value Hierarchies

The great variety of values suggest that they can and must be ranked higher and lower, implying also that the ways, principles, and modalities of ranking values also differ. Preference itself is expressed either as a 'placing before' or as a 'placing after,' thereby distinguishing the enthusiast from the ascetic. The former stresses the positive preferability of one value over others; the latter, the negative, that a given value is less preferable than another. The first smothers vices with virtues; the second strives for virtue by suppressing vice. Neither can be pursued exclusively, though Western psychology is generally more attuned to the positive, enthusiastic method, while Eastern ways tend to stress the negative, ascetic approach. Finally, there is but one ultimate preference principle: an absolute value is preferable to a relative value. The more absolute value leaves the conviction that preferring another to it is to fall from a higher state of value-existence. Since there can be only one absolute value, the intuition into the meaning of infinite being, whether assumed or real, all other values share in absoluteness to the extent they reflect the qualities of infinity (Scheler 1973, 99).

There are four such principles. (1) The more enduring a value, the higher the value. The longer-lasting value is preferred to the transient. The betrothed with his "I love you!" perceives a higher value than the gallant's "You give me pleasure!" (2) The more holistic value is more to be preferred. Spiritual values are to be preferred over material values. Obliterating the smile destroys the Mona Lisa; removing a BMW's carburetor will lessen, not wipe out, its value. (3) The more basic the value, the more it is to be preferred. Health presupposes life, and life—existence. Hence, existence is the deeper and more basic value, just as an eternal and infinite being must be the absolute value. (4) Values yielding deeper contentment are preferable to passing pleasures. Acts of charity are more fulfilling than a night on the town. (Of course, such an evening could be important for other reasons than just pleasure.)

Scheler called the last rules of preferring value modalities (Scheler 1973, 105–10). They are categories of values ranked according to the perception of their absolute or relative goodness. These, as well as the ways of valuing and rules of ranking, are very much dependent on the intuition into one's innate values—the natural tendencies to the goods of life, play, truth, friendship, beauty, religion, practical rationality here, and for an ultimate purpose hereafter. This universal endowment means that, while people will differ in being exposed to more or less dramatic events and associate with more or less important people, all can evaluate people and things with keener or superficial insight depending upon their insights into their own innate values. Value modalities, therefore, are value categories ranked according to the depth of the evaluator's perception/preference of an object's absolute or relative goodness.

At the lowest level the *sensual* values, given in sensations and perceived as yielding pleasure and pain, are ranked across a spectrum from agreeable to disagreeable. True values are, nevertheless, the most transient, partial, and peripheral feeling states. At a higher level, *vital* values, perceived as relating to life and well-being are ranked from lively to lifeless; to plants and animals from peerless to inferior; to equipment and tools from useful to useless. They arouse the feeling-states of gladness to sadness, healthy to ill, successful to failing. At the third level, *spiritual* values, relating to human needs for beauty, knowledge, and goodness, are termed aesthetic and are ranked from beautiful to ugly; intellectual, true to false; and moral, right to wrong. The highest value-modality is the sacred, ranking values from the holy to unholy. It encompasses the other three, since all values ultimately relate to the values of absolute being and goodness. The relation of these modalities to the natural propensities is both obvious and essential for developing one's value hierarchy. The values dominating one's life and action are rooted in one's basic urges and can be classified in any of the value modalities.

Although most people acquire their value systems haphazardly, some purpose is evident in the dominant values at whatever value level. Aesthete, for example, denoting a refined sensuality, is further specified by gourmet in food, connoisseur in drinks, and paramour in sex. Hedonist, glutton, rake, and drunkard describe a gross sensuality. In opposition, austerity is reflected by teetotaler, abstinent, and chaste. Dominating vital values are tallied by the champion in sports, the powerful in politics, the successful in business, the star in entertainment, and hero in feats of daring. Opposing are the failure, powerless, coward, and so forth. Savant suggests someone attuned to artistic and natural beauty. Scholar denotes one keen for knowledge, and benevolent the person seeking the good in all people and things. At the highest level a saint seeks and sees all reality in the light of an infinite and supreme being. Ideally, everyone's value system should tend to peak at a height such as this.

Despite this theoretical order, only the rarest individual manifests a coherent system in his or her ruling values. Most such value systems exemplify the randomness in experiencing persons, circumstances, and events in life. Even so, dominant values are not static but dynamic. About them, lower values, preferences, and wants coalesce. They, in turn, are the source of acts and eventually habits—that is, they tend to become characteristic virtues and vices. At the same time, one's value system experiences pressure from others' value espousals and, mostly, from class or society values, especially when differing from one's own.

All such dynamism suggests that dominant values and the virtues and vices they foster may not be entirely consistent. A person or society may espouse for a long time contrary or even contradictory values and courses of action. Once seen in conflict, they can generate personal or social crises. All told, value hierarchies are complex phenomena. In summary, analysis of values and value systems demonstrates that the value hierarchy corresponds with the organic process of human development. Even though values are perceived immediately and intuitively, a person cannot penetrate to an object's inmost core of good except after years of devoted effort. Striving for higher values and the conduct they mandate is not for the fainthearted nor without consequences for one's life and personality. Dominant values become a person's "deeply propriate dispositions" and "central thrusts of one's striving" (Allport 1965, 454).

Forming the value hierarchy, therefore, embodies personalism by turning an inwardness outward to the world of both matter and spirit and to others' good. Hence it confirms commitment to them and generates a progressive liberation to choose the good. Thus personal and value growth, as organically and creatively interdependent and interacting, form the critical point of the *drama of personhood*. But like any dramatic form, it needs an economic setting and props as secondary but materially essential for the action to develop. This, in turn, implies another kind of value, whose import and meaning, now subsumed under and expressed by the simple term *price*, are products of a long and complex history.

ECONOMIC VALUE

Prices, as cognitive constructs in money form, manifest the exchange or economic value of products and services as they circulate through the economy.

As such, prices are as necessary for human living and social intercourse as personal values. One sure litmus test of value espousal is what a person is willing to pay for the means to achieve it. That is, personal values are, in a sense, priced. Thus, like the family cat and dog, economists and value philosophers must accept their respective validities. This is especially so in that the two analyses start from quite different premises: personalist value theory from intuition into the nature of the human person; economic from experience of the universal and empirical facts of prices. How this value theory developed in response to changing economic conditions over the centuries will reveal its makeup and suggest how it relates to personal values.

Pre-Classical Value Theory

As is often the case, the story begins with Aristotle. While affirming that justice required trading equal for equal, he knew that exchanging unequal amounts of differing goods required some common denominator measurement, which he saw as the community's desire for the good and its producer's function in society. For Aristotle, therefore, economic value expresses and is measured by *community standards* and *needs* (Aristotle 1905, 4–5). Eight hundred years later in a disintegrating Rome, Augustine, the Christian Platonist, affirmed that value in exchange should reflect *people's desires*, not a commodity's intrinsic and essential worth (Augustine 1952, 331a).

Aquinas, aware of the growing interurban and interregional commerce of the thirteenth century, taught that, while the just price should reflect the *common estimate* of producers, consumers, and market regulators, such consensus is never quantitatively precise and varies over time and from place to place (Aquinas II-II 1911, 77). Later moralists, like Scotus, Biehl, Antoninus, and the Jesuits, Molina, Lessius, and de Lugo enriched this just price theory with observations of business practice to develop a comprehensive and sophisticated *supply and demand* value theory. Well into the eighteenth century, the Abbe Galiani (1728–87) held this value theory, which was a century ahead of Quesnay and Smith (Spiegel 1971, 202–5).

Nevertheless, the explosive growth of national economies and international trade shifted interest from concern for justice to analysis of purely secular national economic growth. From crude mercantilistic ideas about favorable trade balances, economists strove to see how economies grew from within by creating *surplus value*. The great works of Petty (1623–87), Cantillon (1685–1734), Quesnay, Smith, Hume, Turgot, Steuart, and others have the common feature of integrating individual motivation and action into a comprehensive schema of national growth. Petty's survey of the Irish economy yielded the conviction that an economy's surplus value can be measured as increases both of resources and of manpower. Cantillon, the Irish-French entrepreneur, systematized this rough outline, placing it within a sociological setting and adding the circulation of money and international trade. The court physician Quesnay then capped their work with his *Tableau Economique*, a circular-flow model of goods and money together generating and dispensing surplus value throughout the economy. Basic to all three is the conception of economic value as the material substratum, *the stuff* which is generated in the primary industries and out of which all useful goods are made.

Quesnay's insightful model of a national economy was fleshed out by two philosopher/friends, David Hume and Adam Smith. Hume sketched in the elements of a dynamic *free-market economy*, showing how international trade, price levels, circulation of money, profits and production, and wages and consumption interacted, each affecting and being affected by the others (Hume: passim). Smith then showed how *exchangeable values*, as kinds of common denominators of all economic goods, are generated at all levels of production and in every industry. Exchangeability itself, when sparked by desires to progress materially, motivates increasing productivity through division of labor, thus accumulating capital, expanding markets, and distributing output more widely. Hence, the generation of exchangeable values naturally harmonizes private gain with public interests, wealth creation with the populace's well-being, industrial progress with agricultural improvement. Exchangeable value, consequently, not only connects all elements of the economy but provides motivation for all economic activity (Smith 1937, bks 1 and 2). Other economic circumstances would reveal other constituents of economic value.

Classical Values and Neo-Classical Synthesis

Three events of seismic proportions marked the first score years of the nineteenth century. The Industrial Revolution was in full swing in England and growing elsewhere; the Napoleonic Wars were over, and that initiated a new surge in population. Altogether they had a revolutionary effect on economic growth and thence on economic value theory. David Ricardo made the most convincing case that *income sharing* is essential for both economic value and economic growth. While the work embodied in products constitutes their real value, capital and natural resources as well as labor must be compensated if the production of reproducible goods were to continue. But because population growth increases the cost of land and other fixed resources, while labor's wages cannot fall below the survival level, and because at the same time increasing output lowers product prices, profits are inevitably squeezed, and output is curtailed as a consequence. Produced values are inadequate to compensate producing values. That is, economic growth by diminishing economic values begets its own demise (Ricardo 1912, chs. 1–8).

This pessimistic conclusion, despite unprecedented economic growth, caused Ricardo's followers and critics to reexamine the production process. Most concluded that the *organic composition* of capital (how work, material, and capital are combined) yielded significantly different value outputs, which must in all cases equal or better the *costs of production*. John Stuart Mill, in summarizing the classical achievement, could hold the paradox of prosperity producing declining values, because he could accept both a no-growth economy and state intervention in the economy (Mill 1848, bk 2, ch. 1, and bk 4). Marx, spurning such compromise, put a *pure labor theory of value* at the center of a revolutionary view of humanity: people both fulfill themselves through work and are united to it by others. Further, since socially necessary labor constitutes a thing's use value and abstract *labor power* its exchange value, labor is the sole source of surplus value. Capital by expropriating this sets in motion the dialectic process which transforms capitalism into communism (Marx 1952, chs. 1–12, 16, 24, 25).

While most economists were struggling with a labor theory of value, a few—Say, Cournot, Gossens, and von Thünen among them—were reviving the neglected concept of utility, the perceived *usefulness* of the good or service itself. Almost as one, Jevons, Menger, and Walras (Schumpeter 1954, 825–9) demonstrated that economic value was determined by the market desire for the good, the exchange rate being the ratio of the additional satisfaction, the *marginal utility* of more of a good, against the opportunity cost of having less from other goods. The values of productive factors are similarly imputed from the ratios of the product's value to the factors' opportunity costs. Thus all values are related both horizontally and vertically in a set of interdependent ratios of exchange rates. Finally, when Marshall integrated the labor theory of value into marginal utility analysis (Schumpeter 1954, 921–4), economics at last could consistently explain the phenomena of value, price, wealth, income, costs, wages, and gain, synthesizing which easily translates into *price theory*. The economy is a self-regulating system.

This simplification opened vast fields of empirical research and a whole new menagerie of price influences: money supply and financial practices, fiscal policy and taxation, advertising and consumer preference, market power and government mediation. It also demonstrates that economic and moral values, despite verbal similarity, differ markedly. Economic value (price) is objective, *quantitative,* and *constraining.* Set by changing market forces, a price, as the ratio of an amount of a commodity to an amount of money, expresses the empirical and mathematical facts which set the terms of trade. As such it gives power: the power to buy.

On the other hand, moral values are *subjective, qualitative,* and *free.* They are, therefore, freely chosen and rated, one value outranking but not excluding others. Perceiving/preferring anything's goodness becomes, given the manner and intensity of its espousal, a personal standard of conduct. This contrast between economic and moral values incline economists, in promoting a science of neat and quantifiable price ratios, to reject that whatever role, even if significant, personal values play in economic decisions, is simply absorbed into price. The only significance of such evaluations for economic analysis is the fact of purchase or not. As a result the role of the person as agent is further excluded from economic analysis.

To the contrary, while price theory with its basic concepts of costs, money, markets, supply and demand, and profits tends to explain the economic process solely in a material and impersonal way, prices actually arose out of centuries of personalist thought: community needs, people's desires, common estimate, exchangeability, labor power and costs, income sharing, and utility. Most personal values, too, inhere in matter which must be worked up by labor and technology and then marketed. Conversely, products and services, though possessing exchange value, have little moral value in themselves. Their principal worth is as means to service more ultimate goals, intentions, and purposes, that is, as values pertaining to a person's role as citizen, as family member, as social being, or to one's dominant values as civil servant, artist or scholar, or as moral being. This fact, that economic values are inextricably involved in values by which persons rule and guide their lives and which become their life's drama, signifies that all economic acts have personal and moral dimensions beyond price, gain, and material betterment for the person himself or herself. As such then they are part and parcel of the human drama.

Just as physicists and biologists found their research could not be divorced from the real world, so more economists are returning to the traditions of economics' founders in giving more consideration to social issues and values. Indeed, they are finding that some of the most controversial topics their science is asked to address, such as economic growth, free enterprise, full employment, social planning, income distribution, environmental protection, and the rest, possess large doses of social and moral values. Thus, how personal values affect economic values and more importantly how generating economic values influences espousing moral and social values must be brought center stage here.

ECONOMIC VALUE IN THE VALUE HIERARCHY

This, in turn, needs some clear distinctions. Economic value is itself bimodal: as exchange value it is simply the good's price, its monetary worth set by the market; but as use value it is both more complex and more clearly related to personal values. Almost everything—natural resources, capital goods, skills, ideas, effort, commodities—has use value, usefulness, or utility. But that is in the eye of the users. When bought, a commodity's full usefulness is not realized but only expected. Also, the amount of a good already had affects the utility of having more, with satisfaction increasing at a marginally decreasing rate, while the satisfaction from goods foregone, their opportunity cost increases at an increasing rate. Conversely, as sales increase, suppliers' opportunity costs decrease and those of competitors' increase, and, of course, vice versa. Finally, producers may incorporate in the product features they hope will sell but buyers see uses the seller never foresaw: beer bottles become table decorations!

All of these factors converge and interact to generate the economic and exchange values of goods and services, that is, their market prices. Altogether they determine the real costs of implementing people's desires and preferences for use-values and also sellers' gains in supplying them.

Seen, however, from the point of view of value theory, use-value is the value-utility. As such it fits into the second tier of Scheler's value hierarchy with the vital and other values relating to and enhancing well-being. Utility, however, is not a good-in-itself but a means-value, a value-for-another-value. As such, utility is anything which helps to achieve another value from the most sensual to the most spiritual. It applies especially to what is produced for sale, prices expressing market and society's preferences. Hence, also, the *value-utility* takes on the coloration of whatever is the user's purpose: the demander's, whether to save his soul or satisfy his lust, and the supplier's, whether to service others' wants or feed a greed for gain, or both.

In turn, the exchange's social context may produce a special effect. Envy and emulation may motivate buying what a person has little use for and less need of, thus yielding more psychic than real use-value. It may even reverse the good's diminishing marginal utility: the more people have of it, the more others want. For suppliers the reverse is true: instead of declining marginal revenue, it increases until competition sates the market and this fad fades like all the others. Such frivolous spending has been condemned as *consumerism*. But its effect as a value problem is worse.

If the public prefers base and lower values over higher and nobler human values, the market will supply the commodities, the use-values to realize them. In this way it happens that the sentimental is preferred to art, the faddish to style, the clever to quality, the slick to honesty, notoriety to character, the superficial to what will endure. As also frequently results, talent, skill and charisma, will be prostituted to market the means to base values. Moreover, the opportunity costs of virtue, honesty, and art may increase not because they are less valued but because their contraries are wanted more. In sum, consumerism, although abetted by the market is more a moral than an economic problem.

With its firm foundation in the hierarchy of values, utility bridges economics and morality. "To adopt a value is to espouse principles of policy in the expenditure of resources" (Rescher 1960, 134). If a person really espouses a value, he or she is willing to make economic sacrifices for the means to achieve it. In this sense all values have a price. *Just as the person is embodied in time and space, so utility as a means-value is embodied in price.* Conversely, and more to the point here, people's value preferences are wholly independent determinants of the prices of the material means to achieve those values.

Affirming this, of course, does not allay the difficulties. It does not say that the intensity of a value espousal is proportional to the price paid for the value's means nor that a person with a fervently held value can always afford the means to it. But it does acknowledge that a price increase of the means does require a stronger espousal and, conversely, that persons who can afford but do not buy the means do not really espouse the value. On the other hand, people distort means-values into final-values when they acquire products and services not for use but for display and ego-inflation. In sum, one of the ultimate tests of a value espousal is to accept the value's opportunity costs among which is paying the prices of the means to the value. In this sense every economic act involves value judgments.

A more telling test is what values, especially the dominant ones, persons bring to producing goods and services. From the start it is conceded that there is no necessary correlation between economic reward and an espoused value's modality. The most endearing value like mother love may be shabbily rewarded while a sleazy comic makes millions. Persons may take dominant values as vocational guides and be rewarded little or late. Others may sacrifice such values for others less desired but more lucrative. For both there are added rewards respectively of contentment or discontent, self-respect or self-loathing.

More destructive of a value system's right order is the metamorphosis of the value-utility from a means value into a goal and purpose of economic action—that is, when a person's purpose changes from providing others' needs and wants and serving the common good to greed for gain and the power wealth bestows. Even worse is when the economy and its institutions are subverted from servicing customers to fostering economic ambition and personal glorification. Such is also the case when subordinates are not respected as coworkers but as thralls of the boss, when office perks are not for facilitating the manager's job but glorifying his eminence, when the latest gadgets and techniques are acquired not as ways to reduce costs but to flaunt the business's ultramodernity, when income and wealth are not put to use to improve business but to evidence the directors' societal superiority, and when the bottom line is not to guide the business but to gratify its executive. All the above suggest how *economic rationality* can be warped by *moral perversion*.

In summary, a personalist view of an economic person's self-awareness, sociality, value seeking, and drive for transcendence confirms the material constraints and limits on people's transpersonal aspirations. More specific analysis of how values are espoused, ranked in a system, and inform behavior was laid out as framework for economic conduct. Since production, exchange, and price are essential for all human activity, the thoughts of economists and philosophers on how economic value, the price system, markets, and trade-offs work explain a necessary, though mediatory, process by which final values are espoused and human purposes achieved.

While economic analysis refers only to physical and temporal goals, nevertheless, since persons, as embodied spirits, can gain their ultimate goal only by material means, all physical actions, including the economic, relate to their espousals and thus their moral lives. Just as a pilot, navigating in midocean with no visible landsites, must fix a course by both longitude and latitude, so an economic person in seeking, using, and enjoying material goods needs both pragmatic economic values and personalist moral values. Economic and personal values, therefore, while distinct, are inseparable, mutually influencing, and gain motivating.

REFERENCES

Allport, Gordon W. *Pattern and Growth in Personality*. New York: Holt, Rinehart, and Winston, 1965.

Angell, Robert C. *Free Society and Moral Crisis*. Ann Arbor, Mich.: University of Michigan Press, 1965.

Aquinas, Thomas. *Summa Theologica*. Translated by the Fathers of the English Dominican Province. New York: Benziger, 1911.

Aristotle. *Nichomachean Ethics*. Translated by W. D. Ross. Oxford: Clarendon, 1905.

Augustine. *The City of God*. Translated by M. Dodds. Chicago: Encyclopedia Britannica, 1952.

Danner, Peter L. "Personalism, Values, and Economic Values," *Review of Social Economy* 40, no. 2 (October 1982).

Finnis, John. *Natural Law and Natural Rights*. Oxford: Clarendon, 1980.

Hume, David. *Writings on Economics*. Edited by E. Rotwein. Madison, Wis.: University of Wisconsin Press, 1930.

Kavanaugh, John F., S.J. *Recovery of Personhood: An Ethics After Post-Modernism*. Milwaukee, Wis.: Marquette University Center for Ethics Studies, 1994.

Marx, Karl. *Capital*. Translated by S. Moore and E. Aveling and edited by Friedrich Engels. Chicago: Encyclopedia Britannica, 1952.

Mill, John Stuart. *Principles of Political Economy*. Boston: Little, Brown, 1848.

Mounier, Emmanuel. *Personalism*. Translated by Phillip Mairet. South Bend, Ind.: University of Notre Dame Press, 1952.

Rescher, Nicholas. *Introduction to Value Theory*. Englewood Cliffs, N.J.: Prentice Hall, 1960.

Ricardo, David. *The Principles of Political Economy and Taxation*. New York: Everyman's Library, 1912.

Scheler, Max. *Formalism in Ethics and Non-formal Ethics of Value: A New Attempt toward the Foundation of Ethical Personalism*. Translated by M. Frings and R. Funk. Evanston, Ill.: Northwestern University Press, 1973.

Schumpeter, Joseph A. *History of Economic Analysis*. Edited from manuscript by E. B. Schumpeter. New York: Oxford University Press, 1954.

Scruton, Roger. *The Aesthetics of Architecture*. Princeton, N.J.: Princeton University Press, 1979.

Smith, Adam. *An Inquiry into the Nature and Causes of the Wealth of Nations*. Edited by Edward Cannan. New York: The Modern Library, 1937.

Spiegel, Henry W. *The Growth of Economic Thought*. Englewood Cliffs, N.J.: Prentice Hall, 1971.

Spranger, Eduard. *Types of Men: The Psychology and Ethics of Personality*. Translated by P. Pigors. Hulle, Saale: M. Niemeyer, 1928.

Teilhard de Chardin, Pierre. *The Divine Milieu*. 1ˢᵗ Perenial Classics Edition. New York, Harper, 1960.

——. *The Phenomenon of Man*. Translated by Bernard Wall. New York: Harper & Row, 1965.

Chapter Seven

Personalism and Gain Seeking

Economic persons as agents are obviously essential to the economy, because they need and want economic goods and services and because they join in the global process of developing Earth's resources and powers to satisfy those same needs and wants. Given that, what faculty in the nature of economic persons makes the economy go? The short answer is that they want to improve their current material well-being and to generate wealth for future wants. That is, they want *to gain*: to get an output they value more than their outlay for it.

The economic person as embodied spirit, of course, needs matter, physical, chemical, and biological objects of the simplest to the complex, in order to survive, grow, and act. Matching such needs, persons are equipped with a marvelous set of faculties to attain them. These range from the vital propensities, like protective reflexes, sexual urges, hungers, and thirsts, to natural appetites for and sensitivity to sound, color, odor, taste, and texture in both their natural states and as fashioned into music, perfume, art, and so forth, and thence to spiritual desires for knowledge, beauty, and goodness. Since all appetites function physically and affect the material universe, when seen empirically from the outside they are called *propensities* or *drives*; when seen from within, intuitively, as satisfying wants, they are termed *appetites*.

Distinct from but tied to sensual appetites is the appetite for wealth. While no less rooted in the person's embodiment in matter, gain seeking as the necessary means to wealth is a calculating appetite. It is the inevitable legacy of the human condition that to desire and have any economic product something must be surrendered. Exchange rationality, therefore, requires that the value of what is acquired should be more than the value of the surrendered good. Since practically everything people desire is obtained by economic actions, most appetitive acts involve two considerations: the want satisfying ability of the wanted good—its desirability—and the cost of sacrificing other wanted but less desired goods.

This view of persons' bilateral bonds to the physical world brings appetitive actions into consideration of both moralists and economists—of economists because physical acts and goods are the substance of the economic process, and of moralists because they pertain to the person's nature and actions as *embodied* spirit. Hence, gain seeking, as the force driving the economy to produce what economic persons want, is the *nexus* that links economic aims and rationality with moral principles and aims. A full understanding of gain seeking, therefore, requires blending moral and economic principles into a unified guide for conduct, which then can be called *economic morality*.

That this conclusion generally evokes an obdurate skepticism is largely due to the long history of contention about the role and importance of gain seeking. Western scholars have for over twenty-five hundred years wrestled with the problem which arises from the differing view of the gain appetite in the moral sciences and actions from that in economic theory and practice. A brief survey of the changing conceptions of gain seeking, when set against the evolving kinds and content of economic wealth, will help toward perceiving gain seeking as a distinct and necessarily propelling faculty of the economic person.

GAIN AND WEALTH IN WESTERN THOUGHT

During the Classical and Medieval periods moralists usually listed gain seeking among the sense appetites because they saw wealth as sensually satisfying, as in *appetitus infinitus divitiarum*, i.e. the unlimited appetite for riches, rather than as something economically productive. This made sense, because most wealth then consisted of lands, dwellings, domestic slaves, apparel, appointments, and hoards of coin. Some wealth, like merchants' workshops, ships and stores, lands, and slaves was working capital. But all forms, even though proof of past gain, were desired more as useful, pleasurable, or bestowing power and prestige. Thus moralists considered them more as sensual goods than as economic objects. Moreover, since there was little financial wealth, which has no sensual appeal and cannot be worked as such but nevertheless changes the ebb and flow of the globe's economic activity, as the jet stream changes the weather, scholars were neither inclined nor saw the need to separate the economic from the sensual aspects of the wealth appetite. Thus gaining as generating economic growth was not apparent as such and thus not considered.

Of the ancients, Plato was most concerned about the evils of sensuality and most inclined to see gain/wealth seeking and the sense and vital appetites as alternately fostering and motivating each other. For him a personal internal harmony requires reason both to control unruly appetites and also to be content with one's economic lot (Plato 1952a, 430–44). In the *Laws*, he argues for limiting both population and personal wealth and restricting net gain seeking, insisting that a stable and moral society is best realized in a zero-growth economy (Plato 1952b, 740–6), that is, one generating no net gain.

Aristotle joins Plato in linking inordinate gain seeking to prodigal acquisitive and sense appetites (Aristotle 1952a, 1107). But he postulates two uses for economic goods and tasks: their primary or proper use, to be produced and consumed in the household so as to satisfy personal wants, and their secondary or subsidiary use, to produce goods for sale or exchange. Thus he differentiates gain seeking somewhat from other appetites (Aristotle 1952a, 1257). But since production is for consumption, income and wealth should be held to what one needs to live well, moderation steering between indulgence and parsimony. Trade, however, since it lacks a natural limit and a defined purpose, is not moral *per se*. Moreover, since wealth can be increased beyond what is sufficient, Aristotle proposes a control. He enlists liberality, as the mean between parsimony and prodigality, to employ surpluses in uses beneficial for others. Hence, Aristotle can tolerate commerce and trade (Aristotle 1952a, bk 4).

The Stoic and Epicurean pragmatic successors of Plato and Aristotle, while disagreeing on basic principles, differed little in ethical practice. A scholar/politician like Cicero reflected both ethics, easily blending Stoic philosophizing with luxurious living and amassing wealth by exploiting provinces. Christians, however, tended to stress the more spartan forms of Stoicism. Indeed, the most faithful exemplars of Epictetus were Christian hermits, fleeing urban decadence. Augustine, the Christian Platonist, shocked by the Vandals' sack of imperial Rome, warns the faithful on journey to the City of God against setting their hearts on worldly pleasures, using but not indulging in the good things it offers (Augustine 1952, 625). It reflects his suspicion of what he considers the general business principle, to buy cheap and sell dear. The view of most moralists that merchants seldom, if ever, are pleasing to God was corroborated by their censure of usury as a costless gain from others' needs (Noonan 1957, IV and V). Together they meant that an "infinite appetite for riches" so reeked of brimstone and fire that cautious merchants would hedge bets on the hereafter with deathbed donations to charity and masses for their souls.

Following Augustine and Aristotle, Aquinas condemns greed for gain as a root of moral evil, since money is universally desired as means for all appetites

(Aquinas I–II 1920, q. 84, a.1). He echoes Aristotle that unlimited seeking of wealth denotes a disordered concupiscence and its tendency to excess violates both justice and moderation. Aquinas does recognize the benefits of trade and approves profits earned justly and used to subserve one's family or the common good (Aquinas I–II 1920, q.77, a.4). This mild concession to profits helped nudge Medieval moralists toward grudgingly accepting, or tolerating economic gain.

But Henry of Hesse (1325–97) more typically represents the general suspicion of gain seeking: "He who has enough to satisfy his wants and nevertheless ceaselessly labors to acquire riches . . . (is) incited by a damnable avarice, sensuality, and pride (Tawney 1926, 36). Such suspicion of trade endured right into the sixteenth century. Even Cajetan (1470–1534), the great commentator of Aquinas' *Summa*, conceded that banking and other business, while not licit *per se*, could be so only "if ordained to the decent support of one's family and status" (Noonan 1957, 313).

The Disengagement of Gain Seeking

John Calvin (1509–64) was among the first to part this cloud of suspicion. Despite his dogma of salvation by predestination, Calvin held that, while people could not be saved through good works, they could not be saved without them (Calvin 1960, 798). Like his contemporaries condemning usury and business injustice, especially to the poor, Calvin preached that accepting life's vocation meant being industrious, frugal, and sober, using and enjoying in moderation life's pleasures (Calvin 1960, 719–25). In Geneva, which he governed like a theocracy, banning both dishonesty and license, Calvinism became a blueprint for economic success.

The later Puritan essayist Richard Steele (1672–1729), in his *Tradesman Calling*, is more explicit. Tawney's quotation of Steele is right to the point. "Next to saving his soul, (the merchant's) care and business is to serve God in his calling, *and to drive it as far as it will go*" (emphasis added) (Tawney 1926, 246). Montesquieu, the French political theorist, (1689–1755) carried this precept beyond the Calvinist sphere, affirming that people "may acquire vast riches without corruption of morals . . . because the spirit of commerce is naturally attended with that of frugality, economy, moderation, labor, patience, order, and rule" (Montesquieu 1949, 46).

In England this conclusion provided a comfortable conscience for scholars celebrating Britain's expanding commercial empire (Roll 1961, 55–138). Gain seeking, as affecting national aspirations, begot political economy. Sir Joshua Child (1630–99) saw England as "wonderfully fitted by the bounty of

God Almighty for a great progression in wealth and power" (Child 1693, Preface). Mandeville (1678–1733) went even further in arguing that sensuality, greed, and ambition beget prosperity, while frugality and sobriety cause depression (Mandeville 1723). His cynical sophistry set off the altruism/ egoism debate over economic self-interest, which engaged the age's leading moralists, including David Hume and Adam Smith.

Paralleling this was the refinement of both private gain and national economic growth from the Mercantilist "overvent" to the Physiocratic "net product" and to the Classicist "surplus value." Then Quesnay's conception of countering product and money flows locates the economy's driving force mainly in the self-interest of entrepreneur/farmers by whose enterprise the *stuff* of material wealth is increased (Schumpeter 1959, 233–43). Next David Hume negates Mandeville: "It is an infallible consequence of industrious professions to beget frugality and make love of gain prevail over the love of pleasure" (Hume 1930, 53). Finally, Smith, though milder, formulated the gain principle which is still quoted: "The desire to better our condition, which, though generally calm and dispassionate, comes with us from the womb, and never leaves us till we go into the grave" (Smith 1952, 147). Thus private gaining as by an Invisible Hand becomes the instrument of economic growth.

While Smith assumed that economic justice normally prevailed, his followers' uncontested faith in the Invisible Hand tended to disengage gain seeking from the other appetites and to free it from moral control. Since also Smith's economic self-interest requires mutuality, reciprocity, and harmonizing economic goals, Smith's heirs inferred that gain seeking by itself can promote the public good. Thus they usually ignored the need for moral principles and tutelage. Gain maximization, in being stripped of moral implications, becomes in Classical and later Neoclassical analysis an amoral human propensity and a common sense economic principle, a premise for choosing among alternatives. No longer an appetite, it is free of moral control. Some even made it the foundation of moral action.

Nassau Senior (1790–1864), in inaugurating Political Economy at Oxford in 1825, recalled Hume's affirmation that gain seeking itself is the most effective moral principle. Senior said, "The pursuit of wealth, that is the endeavor to accumulate the means of future subsistence and enjoyment, is to the mass of mankind the great source of moral improvement" (Senior 1827, 12). Imagine his shock at Newman's bitter denunciation that his remark was "so very categorical a contradiction of our Lord, St. Paul, St. Chrysostom, St. Leo, and all the Saints" (Newman 1947, 81). This still is the root difference today between moralists and economists over gain seeking. However, the gain principle was to encounter difficulties from both economists and other scientists.

Problems of an A-Moral Gain

Simultaneous with the disengagement of gain seeking from the sense appetites and the 'demoralization' of the wealth and gain incentive was the vast increase in production and capital goods, *working wealth*, which the Industrial Revolution generated. That, in turn, resulted in further difficulties in accepting the gain principle. Probably the most enduring concern is that gain seeking and profit seeking inevitably generate slowdowns and even economic stagnation. This idea, first advanced in Ricardo's taut logic, that increased output increased costs and decreased prices, thus reducing both profits and production, (Ricardo 1963, chs. 1–8) revived regularly at every recession in the 150 years since Ricardo. Marx went further, predicting that the capitalist compulsion for surplus value (profits) would inevitably convert Capitalism into Communism (Roll 1961, 251–97). Countering him, Social Darwinists argued that both economic liberty and economic growth demanded unrestricted private property, uncurbed competition, and, most of all, an absolute right to gain (Hofstadter 1955).

Economists since then continue to differ over gain seeking, some defending it as the universal cure-all, others as the cause of every ill besetting economies. Despite its role as an amoral economic principle, a moral streak of varying shades has tinted arguments for and against gain seeking. John Stuart Mill would restrict legislation apropos the licitness of gain seeking to protecting the rights of others (Mill 1952, 304–12). Hegel is more statist in asserting society's right and duty to substitute communal goals for personal extravagance (Hegel 1973, 148). By listing profits' evils, Tawney undermined its moral sanction and endorsed the program of Fabian Socialists to control profits by unionization, industrial democracy, taxation, and nationalization (Tawney 1921).

This quite schizoid rejection of moral, while seeking social, controls has recently become more technical. For Keynes it was euthanasia of the rentier; for Schumpeter decline in the spirit of innovation; for Meadows limits to growth; for Georgescu-Roegen entropic degradation. Economists, often joined by scholars from the physical, moral, social, and health sciences, have predicted every kind of catastrophe: global warming, energy entropy, waste of natural resources, atmospheric pollution, population growth beyond Earth's productivity, and others. Doomsayers from acorns of fact have harvested forests of fears. (After an initial stir such prophets of doom usually settle to courting only their true believers.) But all of this reflects a kind of materialistic or a-moral morality, aimed most often at profits, that form of gain which produced wealth worldwide and changed its content and form in just two centuries of the most dynamic economic growth in the history of humankind. This is really one of the unique contributions of Western civilization.

Furthermore, most wealth has been 'de-materialized.' Unlike in earlier economies, most wealth now has little sensual content or appeal. While the wealthy still live grandly, the larger part of great fortunes and of even modest estates today consists in rights to dividends, interests, royalties, pensions, and claims to income and property, which, though greatly desired, are not sensually pleasurable. (Much requires tiresome care to preserve.) Further, most wealth now consists in rights to and control of capital goods, which need others' gain seeking collaboration. Then, too, money has lost its materiality — now almost all of it is bank credit — and near-money is the credit of other financial institutions, giving the credit-worthy further purchasing power.

All told, this means that even large fortunes may not be devoted to support sybaritic living and may be subject to radical change, to both of which the gain appetite may contribute. All advises analyzing further the economics of gain seeking.

THE ECONOMICS OF GAIN

Though the history of gain seeking may seem to have produced the conundrum that, while economic growth is welcome, individual gain seeking is suspect, the controversies and varying opinions of scholars have, like pieces of a mosaic, achieved a discernible pattern. (1) Since the very rationale of the economic process is to exchange what is less desired, less useful, and more plentiful for what is more desired, more useful, and less plentiful, gain seeking must drive economic growth and thus benefit its agents. (2) Though personal, the gain appetite has a social side. By requiring all to participate in producing and sharing the economy's output, it involves everyone in the economic process and price system. (3) While distinct from the sense and vital appetites, gain seeking relates to them as vital for economic persons to survive, grow, and act. Each needs more elaboration. Thus the analysis will first discuss gain seeking as a universal personal drive, putting off discussing its role in driving economic institutions to the next chapter.

Gain Seeking

Gaining implies getting or winning, achieving a good despite difficult circumstances or competition. It is essential in the economy because practically nothing is free. To gain, therefore, is to realize a benefit greater than the cost, usually the price paid to get it. Gain seeking, therefore, in implementing price rationing has an efficiency function, alleviates wanting, and in general counters the tendency to overspend income. Also, just as prices ration goods and services by limiting wanting to what is currently available, so gain encourages and rewards suppliers of goods to provide more. Conversely, what is 'price-less,' or free, encourages extravagant use and discourages production. In short, economic efficiency needs all to seek gain. Whether as consumer, worker, or investor, persons act rationally by trading what they value less for what they want and value more. In this sense, gain seeking permeates the economy as its driving force.

Gain has two features: it arises from property transfers, and by involving exchange values (usually money or near-money) gain produces an effect of some duration. (This excludes barter when goods are exchanged for their use value only: each barterer may be better off but neither acquires exchange value.) Quite the opposite occurs in transfers of paper wealth—mortgages, bonds, stocks, options, and so forth—since traders there are concerned only with ratios of present to anticipated exchange values. For that reason, trading there can yield huge profits and losses of exchange values.

Better known are the exchanges that occur during the course of producing goods and services for final sale. Throughout this long and progressive chain various human and natural use values are traded for exchange values, until in a final sale the good's use value is traded for exchange value (money). At each stage in this chain, profits, as lasting acquisitions of exchange value, must be realized or the production chain might be broken. All this makes obvious common sense. (The matter of unjust or excessive profits will be raised later.)

While profit is the most apparent and controversial form of gain seeking, there are two other lesser known but all-pervasive kinds, consumer surplus and economic rent. The first arises when a product or service is sold to a final user, who prefers the commodity's use value to the exchange value (money) given for it. This is most apparent with bargains, when the price is less than anticipated or more than what the buyer is willing to pay, thus generating residues of exchange value, which can be saved or spent elsewhere. But every purchase, by the very fact of its reasonableness, generates consumer surplus. Economic rent is like this on the side of production, being the difference in exchange value between the price a productive good or labor is paid and what their owners would have taken. Like bargains, economic rent is thus another kind of gain.

Thus the three forms of gain seeking—profits, economic rent, and consumer surplus—match the three moments of economic growth: consumption, production, and investment/enterprise. Every economic person is a consumer, most engage in production, and a growing number (a majority in the richest nations) are investors. Altogether they generate the action/reaction/interaction dynamic of the economic triangle of *consumption*, as end and purpose of the process; of *production*, as means to consumption; and of *investment/enterprise*, the creative risk-taking linking the two. Throughout, persons as agents are activated by gain seeking, just as every cell in the human body is driven by its vital principle to perform whatever role or functions it is ordained to do. In sum, therefore, the economy is driven by gain, and economic persons as economic agents must be gain-seekers. *No gain, no growth is a basic economic rationale.*

(It should be mentioned, as an aside, that all economic gain bears a penumbra of social loss. Every economic good is attended with entropic consequences: every use of energy results in some dissipation, energy which is not reclaimable in useful form; all human acts, even dying, pollute the human habitat in some way, industry causing most; all production and consumption generate garbage and waste, the residue of useful things which cannot be put to use completely. All require compensatory spending. But countering these are benefits beyond immediate gain but due to gain seeking: inventive research, adroit technology, shrewd management, honed skills, and wise investment, all driven by gain seeking, that is, getting more from less.)

Finally, since gain yields a residue of exchange values and wealth a store of exchange values, and since both are usually expressed in money terms, they are price phenomena. That is, gain is but a price differential and wealth simply an accumulation of prices. In this sense, gaining and pricing are inherently linked, each complementing the other: wherever price, there gain—or loss. It requires a closer look at gain and gaining as money and price phenomena.

Gain, Money, and Price

That gain, whether profit, consumer surplus, or economic rent, is a money phenomenon is rather obvious. But not so evident is the social nature of gaining. Because it usually involves money, gain affects more than immediate buyers and sellers, since money and, consequently, pricing affect a social universe as wide and complex as national and global economies. Money, as Ingham suggests, originates deep in human social history. "Monetary [and price] systems are the result of the long-term historical development of a complex structure of social relations and practices" (Ingham 1996, 516).

Suffice it here to see that prices are values expressed in money terms. For most this would only mean commercial and economic exchanges of goods, services, debts, and the like. But prices and quasi prices are central to social functions other than trade and production, such as taxes, fines, assessments, forfeitures, judgments, grants, awards, and rewards, plus the wages and salaries of millions of public and private employees, whose services are appraised and compensated not only for their economic but their social value and worth. (That public servants are paid mainly for their social, not economic, worth helps many avoid penury!) That money payments or penalties should match the social esteem of the parties involved has deep roots in tribal and communal societies and, though seldom acknowledged, is very much operational today.

Like so many of the most basically practical principles for living, the concepts of price and quasi price are owing to no one, but rather evolved as pragmatically needed for social relations and for production and trade. First of all, it is obvious that prices and price changes do not affect a good's function and the benefit or pleasure it gives. Also, products and services that require costlier components and skills command higher prices and play to wealthier clients. Though goods for sale will shift from market to market, products seldom move from high- to low-price markets: canoes do not compete with yachts. While haggling over price generally has little effect on the exchange values economic persons place on goods and services, prices are a major means by which the economy organizes the material texture of living by rewarding and penalizing personal economic acts and the products marketed.

While immaterial and imperceptible, prices are mathematical, measurable, and regulative. All told, prices are odd realities: circumstantial rather than intrinsic, functional rather than essential, conceptual rather than concrete. Indeed, like words, prices are *cognitive constructs*, evoked mentally to measure and define real acts of exchange and to evaluate one's material well-being. Prices, therefore, are not only means of exchange and units of account, but above all are measures of the values people as a society place on economic products and services. Just as thoughts and feelings need and use words and language, prices are the essentially quantitative and social manifestations of intercourse between and among economic persons.

As with literature, economics has created a vast vocabulary of prices to express not only individual exchanges, but price trends, relations, statistics, probabilities, and indexes. Gain itself is the difference between two prices or price sets. Wealth is the total prices one's current property can command in the market; income is the stream of prices received over a given period; employment is human activity assessed by a price. In sum, prices are the raw material of economic science. Although adding nothing useful or desirable to economic goods, prices still guide production and consumption and are, therefore, *the unique objects of gain seeking*. That prices and gains are present in all phases of persons' material being directs this analysis to examine them from a personalist point of view.

A PERSONALIST GAIN SEEKING

As the economy's drive, gain seeking is subject to economic analysis. But also, while its propensity toward physical objects differs from that of the sense appetites, still like them it is subject to moral criteria: justice because others are necessarily involved, and moderation because gains, wealth, money, and prices are all means, not ends, and thus can be excessively desired and immoderately used, when sought for themselves only.

Some preliminary comments are needed here since the subject of appetites, drives, and propensities opens vistas of psychological discussion and research. Here most of this can be skirted by sticking with the relevant facts of human experience, that people have propensities for various things and have built-in capacities or organic adaptations that are connatural to and receptive of different aspects of objects. The eye, for example, is adapted to sense color, sex organs to mate, the mind to know. In turn no appetite, vital, sensory, or spiritual, acts in isolation, the brain marvelously combining their separate impressions into unified perceptions.

A final comment advises that pleasure, howsoever rewarding or motivating, is never the real object of appetency. Aristotle insists that pain and pleasure are not an appetite's purpose and end but supervene in completing the act (Aristotle 1952a, 1174). Pain and pleasure, therefore, while important adjuncts, are only barometers of appetites' operations, pleasure signifying that an appetite is functioning well on an appropriate object. Pain, on the other hand, suggests some malfunctioning or pathology or may be the cost for curing the same. Pain/pleasure functions become dramatically clear, when appetites by over-indulging even their proper objects yield not pleasure but discomfort and pain.

These general observations should help to differentiate the gain propensity from the sense and vital appetites. Accordingly, gain seeking will be distinguished by its unique object and its percipient organ or faculty, by how it is generated and develops, by the excesses to which it tends and how they are controlled.

The Gain Appetite

Gain, while indicating that scarce material goods, services, properties, contracts, and money have been acquired, is itself immaterial, being a mathematical and relational reality. Able to yield much gratification, still it is devoid of sensible and perceptive qualities. As the difference between two sets of prices, it is generated in and by the very act of seeking it in exchange itself. Thus gain, as a socio/economic mental construct, suggests that gain seeking is a function of a faculty by which persons compare, balance, and calculate what is obtained against what must be given. Since gain itself is devoid of material and sensual qualities, the gain appetite functions through a mental, not a physical faculty. In fact, gain seeking is an act of the practical intellect, the ability to grasp factual situations and relations and to act accordingly, as opposed to theorizing about the same.

Since economic growth is universally desired, a minimal gain seeking is required of all but the totally incapable. That drive, therefore, will vary greatly from person to person. It can begin to function in young children, but generally only after tutoring about "the value of a dollar" and living within a budget will the gain appetite become truly operational. Given the fluidity of prices, the transience of wealth, and the volatility of gain, it usually needs years of training and cultivation before it becomes for most the rational and sophisticated instrument of the economically successful. Still, some have honed it to a keenness that they seem almost to smell gain, bargains, deals, and profits. Acuity of the gain instinct explains as well as, if not more so than family fortune or luck, the differences in today's economic success.

Further, gain seeking is potentially keener than most sense and vital appetites because the objects sought are more universal. Money, economic values, gain, profits, income, and wealth are all generic goods, exchangeable for many things or saved. The objects of sense and vital appetites, on the other hand, are specific: this minivan, this steak, which once possessed or consumed cease to be such objects. But more income is always welcome, and wealth, especially paper wealth, can be increased indefinitely because the owners are not compelled to spend it. Kept for future eventualities, wealth gives power: purchasing power and thus prestige. In short, gain seeking can become an all-consuming drive.

The preceding makes clear that gain seeking, when its natural drive becomes excessive or addictive, presents considerable moral danger. Wealth accumulation is not like other appetites subject to physical satiation: wealth can be and often is amassed beyond what is moderately beneficial or gained justly. Rather like a collector's mania, gaining much is likely to stimulate the desire for more, neither age nor declining physical powers abating the greed for gain. Finally, in free market economies wealth addiction, unlike addictions to drugs, alcohol, or other vices, does not bring social obloquy but rather increased social respectability. Great wealth, no matter how acquired, usually trails an aura of social respect. Hence the paradox that objects with no sensual appeal may generate irresistible desires, the infinite appetite of Scholastic ethics. Clearly, such a powerful drive with all its social consequences needs built-in controls and moral principles.

Most people are required to exercise some control over their gain seeking, since they must function competitively in a social matrix. Also, while gain seeking is self-interested, it is not solely self-serving. Like cells in the body, persons acting as economic agents willy-nilly serve the economic common good by seeking gain. Indeed, economic, and moral means are available to moderate excessive gain seeking.

Gain Seeking as Social

Economic competition is the most effective external control over the gain drive. Unlike other kinds of competition — sports, politics, bingo — it is not just a win/lose contest. One wins by offering more or better service or products to customers than do others: thus buyers reciprocate sellers', and sellers buyers', gain seeking. Since competitors in economic exchange mutually constrain each other, gain competition is probably the most effective way of broadly sharing economic well-being and calming most peoples' hopes and ambitions. Moreover, producing for sale almost always requires organizing the skills, resources, and money of others, whose gain desires must be serviced. The clearest evidence of an economy lacking effective competition is one split between the few who live luxuriously and the masses who are destitute.

Realism demands acknowledging, however, that the desire for gain and wealth can become a powerful aphrodisiac, which inherent social brakes cannot control. Most crime in the world is driven by greed for wealth and gain. It is confirmed by tales of lofty aspirations yielding to materialistic ambitions and eventually malpractice, economic crimes blighting successful careers. Many a modern Midas's greed for profits has transformed the spirit of cooperative enterprise into the cold clash of competing desires. (Nothing sets workers' teeth more on edge than denying increases in wages while awarding bonuses to managers and big dividends to stockholders.) Time and again, greed for gain has destroyed the very business that was the source of gain. Again the old adage applies: Whom the gods would destroy they first make mad!

All suggest the need for the personal restraints which moral virtues, especially justice and moderation, offer. In this sense gain seeking as an appetite is no different than other appetites whose excesses harm both the good sought and the seeker. On the other hand, moral control, by reinforcing how competition, cooperation, and collaboration can curb gain seeking, may even at the cost of temporary benefits and seemingly against self-interests insure a longer and more profitable business life.

Surprising to most, the social nature of economic processes is manifested clearly in that gain seeking is self-interested. In preferring some of one thing over an amount of another, which is the essence of property transfers or hiring/proffering labor, the trading parties must consult their own interests. But that does not mean exclusively self-serving. Rather, exchange requires each being alert to the other's interests. Thus Adam Smith: "It is not from the benevolence of the butcher . . . that we expect our dinner, but from [his] regard for [his] own interest" (Smith 1937, 14). His *Moral Sentiments* more clearly asserts that self-concern does not exclude wishing to benefit others: "How selfish soever man be supposed, there are evidently some principles in his nature, which *interest* him in the fortune of others, and render their happiness necessary to him, though he derives nothing from it except the pleasure of seeing it" (Smith 1853, 1) [emphasis added].

Smith saw what many miss today: that self-interest, while it can be selfish, in itself only means an agent has some concern and stake in the act and sees some good forthcoming for self, others, or both. Self-interest, therefore, is not radically egoistic but easily embraces both altruism and benevolence.

In fact, a cursory examination of property transfers reveals a continuum of changing possession from *theft* at one extreme to *trade* and then to *gift* at the other with unnumbered combinations in between. Stealing is the least socially beneficial because what the thief gains net of the costs of stealing and the possibilities of penalties are less than what the owner loses. (Stealing as a dire necessity will be addressed in a moment.) Economic exchange, the most frequent form of property transfer, if uncoerced, is always socially beneficial because while buyer may gain more than seller or vice versa, both gain more than they surrender. (A coerced exchange, of course, is a form of stealing!) The most socially beneficial is the gift, especially when the gift is what the beneficiary truly needs and wants. (Sue shows her appreciation for Grandma's paying her tuition by making Phi Beta Kappa.) Stealing in a matter of dire necessity, food when starving or water to douse a fire, can be assumed to be donated by the owner if the circumstances were known.

The conclusions are obvious: injustice always diminishes the net social benefit of property transfers, and generosity benefits the most when it is effectively used. Similar results are obtained in the hiring of human services and talents: slavery is the least efficient, voluntary service the most so, and uncoerced employment the most usual and in balance the most efficient and beneficial.

To work out in detail all the factors needed to moderate the gain appetite would take volumes. But accepting economic agents as persons and economic conditions as elements of the human state is preliminary. Seeing all economic persons as social will help to regard gain as socially produced and to acknowledge every collaborator's right to share it. Such, in turn, will provide the ground rules for economic justice, market fairness, and thus sound industrial relations. Finally, considerations that gain, devoid in itself of use or pleasure, is but a means to other goods can encourage directing economic ambition to ends and purposes, which by transcending materialistic purposes help people fulfill their careers and vocations as persons.

However one may want to pursue the ideas economic morality and a personalist view of economics propose, the trail starts with realizing that the pursuit of gain is both what economists have brought to light, the motive force driving the economy, and what philosophers have always held, a powerful appetite, which is now differentiated from other appetites. Given this nexus, both moral and economic principles not only can but should be worked into a consistent attitude toward and a behavioral guide for one's gain seeking. The next chapter will continue the discussion of gain and gain seeking as integral to all economic institutions and communities.

REFERENCES

Aquinas, Thomas. *Summa Theologica.* Translated by the Fathers of the English Dominican Province. New York: Benziger, 1920.

Aristotle. *Nicomachean Ethics.* Translated by W. D. Ross. Great Books of the Western World Series edited by Robert Maynard Hutchins. Chicago: Encyclopedia Britannica, 1952.

———. *Politics.* Translated by B. Jowett. Great Books of the Western World Series edited by Robert Maynard Hutchins. Chicago: Encyclopedia Britannica, 1952.

Augustine. *On Christian Doctrine.* Translated by J. F. Shaw. Great Books of the Western World Series edited by Robert Maynard Hutchins. Chicago: Encyclopedia Britannica, 1952.

Calvin, John. *Institutes of the Christian Religion.* Edited by J. R. McNeil and translated by F. L. Battles. Library of Christian Classics, vol. 20. Philadelphia: Westminster, 1960.

Child, Sir Joshua. *A New Discourse of Trade.* London: John Everingtam, 1693.

Danner, Peter L. *An Ethics for the Affluent.* Lanham, Md.: University Press of America, 1980.

———. *Getting and Spending: A Primer in Economic Morality.* Kansas City, Mo.: Sheed and Ward, 1994.

———. "Gain-Seeking: The Econo-Moral Nexus." *Social Economics: Premises, Findings, and Policies.* Edited by E. J. O'Boyle. New York: Routledge, 1996.

Hegel, G. W. F. *The Philosophy of Right.* Translated by T. M. Knox. London: Oxford University Press, 1967.

Hofstadter, Richard. *Social Darwinism in American Thought.* Boston: Beacon Press, 1955.

Hume, David. "A Treatise on Human Nature" and "Of Interest." *Writings on Economics.* Edited by E. Rotwein. Madison, Wis.: University of Wisconsin Press, 1930.

Ingham, Geoffrey, "Money is a Social Relation." *Review of Social Economy* 54, no. 4 (1996): 507–29.

Mandeville, Bernard. *Fable of the Bees.* 2d ed. London, 1723.

Mill, John Stuart. *On Liberty*. Great Books of the Western World Series edited by Robert Maynard Hutchins. Chicago: Encyclopedia Britannica, 1952.

Monroe, A. E. *Early Economic Thought: Selections from Economic Literature Prior to Adam Smith*. Cambridge, Mass.: Harvard University Press, 1951.

Montesquieu, Charles L. *The Spirit of the Laws*. Translated by T. Nugent. New York: Hefner, 1949.

Newman, John Henry. *The Idea of a University*. New York: Longmans, Green, 1947.

Noonan, John T. *The Scholastic Analysis of Usury*. Cambridge, Mass.: Harvard University Press, 1957.

Plato. *The Republic. The Dialogues of Plato*. Translated by B. Jowett. Great Books of the Western World Series edited by Robert Maynard Hutchins. Chicago: Encyclopedia Britannica, 1952a.

Plato. *Laws. The Dialogues of Plato*. Translated by B. Jowett. Great Books of the Western World Series edited by Robert Maynard Hutchins. Chicago: Encyclopedia Britannica, 1952b.

Ricardo, David. *The Principles of Political Economy and Taxation*. Homewood, Ill.: Richard D. Irwin, 1963.

Roll, Eric. *A History of Economic Thought*. London: Faber and Faber, 1961.

Schumpeter, Joseph A. *History of Economic Analysis*. Edited from manuscript by E. B. Schumpeter. New York: Oxford University Press, 1959.

Senior, Nassau. *An Introductory Lecture on Political Economy*. London: J. Mawman, 1827.

Smith, Adam. *An Inquiry into the Nature and Causes of the Wealth of Nations*. Edited by E. Cannan. New York: The Modern Library, 1937.

———. *The Theory of Moral Sentiments*. London: Henry G. Bohn, 1853.

Tawney, R. H. *The Acquisitive Society*. London: G. Bell and Sons, 1921.

———. *Religion and the Rise of Capitalism: A Historical Study*. New York: Harcourt, Brace, 1926.

Chapter Eight

Personalism and Economic Community

This chapter sets itself the anomalous task of demonstrating that self-interested gain seeking is essential to economic *sociality*, which, as an essential ingredient of economic community, is a cement holding economic institutions together. This chapter and the next, therefore, present the economy as neither a free-for-all smorgasbord nor the egalitarian rationing of an authoritarian state, but as a process that reflects both economic persons' individuality and their sociality. That is, everyone by the fact of human conception is individuated and unique only in being related physically to every person who is, was, or will be.

But more so humans relate to each other as persons. 'We,' signifying shared nature, is as common in discourse as 'I.' Other persons and the values they manifest are windows by which to compare one's self. But human sociality means actual physical, purposive, and mental contacts with other people. Such happen daily, times beyond counting, to all but the most reclusive people. Most such events are accidental relations, external, and unintended. Usually they mean little, like sharing an elevator with strangers, but some can be life changing, like an automobile accident. The most important social relations, however, are intended.

These are persons' inherent and essential links to each other owing to their natures as embodied spirits. In fact, for people to grow as persons, maintain public peace and order, and provide the material goods necessary for survival, they must form associations with others. The best known are personal, willed ties, such as husband/wife, doctor/patient, and teacher/student. But public order no less requires a complex net of human relations: legislator/constituents, official/citizens, judge/prisoners, and others. The economy is also woven of human ties: buyers/sellers, employers/employees, lenders/borrowers, and investors/entrepreneurs.

Unlike fleeting external, incidental, and unintended relations, essential relations establish a certain permanence because they generate a common good. The common good of the wife/husband bond, for example, is a shared living that is differently cherished by each. The relation changed to mother/father, their children as mutual goods can convert their union into the family institution. Similarly, teacher/student relations, with their specific common goods of shared learning, generate schools, and politician/citizen beget political parties and governments. So, too, economic acts among persons as gain seekers have developed into the complex institutions of today's industrial economies.

HUMAN ECONOMIC RELATIONS

The impersonality of the market is a favorite theme, not only of many economists but of media commentators for whom GDP, Dow-Jones, rate of unemployment, and so on, tell the economy's real story. But as a matter of fact, every economic act involves persons and specifically those seeking material betterment. For the myriad small businesses, all essential functions are managed in obviously personal ways. But even in megacorporations, operating under the fiction of legal personality, power to act in the corporate's name may be exercised by many persons, even the lowest paid. Such economic relations should not be called impersonal but better identified as complex, since ultimate agents act by way of intermediaries, lines of governance, and sources of information. No matter how complex the business, good management requires definite channels of authority.

Given such complexities, modern corporations, which function in many areas and under diverse political arrangements, require a range of personal skills and knowledge. Consequently, today's business world displays an array of corporate alignments, organizational structures, industry associations, worker organizations, managerial philosophies, and social policies.

Nevertheless, this complexity can be reduced to four fundamental business functions: producing, selling, innovating, and borrowing/lending. Each relates persons as gain seekers; each generates a common good. The product is the common good of the employer/employee relation. For it the worker surrenders time, effort, and skill for income, while the employer provides money, materials, and equipment to obtain a saleable good. The sale then relates buyers and sellers by means of exchange, a mutual gaining in which each surrenders a good less wanted for a good more wanted.

Both functions suggest the need to innovate, the ongoing process of scanning technology for better productive methods, and the market for better ways and products to please customers. The partnership between innovator and investor, generating a new or enhanced enterprise, is probably the most personal of business relationships and requires considerable business trust. This, of course, is an element in every economic act but is most required in the act of borrowing/lending. Here those with wealth to spare surrender it temporarily to those needing it for consumption, production, or investment, interest being charged. Despite the fact that philosophers and theologians debated the morality of taking interest for centuries, today's global financial and banking industry actually has it roots in religious institutions, pagan shrines and temples, monasteries, and religious orders. (They enjoyed the trust, essential for any borrowing or wealth-keeping function.) Business credit—business trust—the common good borrowing/lending creates, is so pervasive today that it is now money and the most used medium of exchange.

Thus personal and intentional relations are fundamental to all economic activity and no more so than the highly publicized activities of giant corporations trying to dominate a market, bidding to take over another or fighting off the same. There the egos, hostility, and truculence of the human contestants are for all to see. In short, while it must be conceded that economic quantification is both possible and necessary to analyze the economy, human motivation from that of householders doing their shopping to that of CEOs plotting their next moves is integral to understanding how the economy functions in a personalist way.

Consequently, personal relations are integral to economic institutions. Given economic scarcity, not so much dearth as the needs engendered by the embodied spirit to feel more, to possess more, and to want better, economic persons must relate with each other to produce and exchange goods and services, to generate new ways of doing so, and to lend their surpluses, always expecting to improve their physical well-being. But individuals seldom act alone; even free-wheeling spirits like celebrated tycoons or industrialists need organizations to effect their visions or depredations. That is, the economy is driven by institutions more than by individuals, except as individuals are incorporated into businesses, corporations, foundations, and so on. Consequently, the economic process, as a fundamental social liturgy, spawns a vast array of interacting economic institutions from charitable societies to cultural and humanitarian associations to profit-seeking enterprises.

Despite their diversity, all economic groupings have much in common. All must produce a good or service that they can sell or for which they can solicit contributions. All must be alert and open to change so that they can borrow or appeal to peoples' generosity when new programs or new technologies require additional funding. In a certain sense all economic institutions must be profit seeking. Even a charity cannot regularly give more than it receives, and must realize that employees, no matter how highly motivated, work to improve their economic condition. Furthermore, the economic institution, whatever its business or mission, must appreciate not only what organizations are competitive with it but which are complementary to it. Finally, its internal structure must manifest a spirit of cooperation and collaboration among its employees and, where possible, some sense of community.

Community as the Ideal Sociality

Community in its various degrees is a condition so important for any organization of human persons, so a short digression to discuss it is worth the effort.

Community is often thought of as neighborhood, especially if one is recalling a childhood among neighbors of the same social status who were aware of and responsive to each others' needs. But the essence of true community, more than neighborliness, is a sense of belonging, uniting a group of people to espouse common values and to act together. As such community is ideal human sociality.

While members may experience different levels of fulfillment, the paradigm community for indigenous people is the tribe or clan village to which all, however important or compatible, belong. In more complex societies it is the nuclear family of parents, children, and often of near kinfolk. Such community is supplemented by many specialized communities, people joining to further their interests in religion, knowledge, politics, sports, business, or other areas.

While value sharing is the cement setting community, at the heart of community is the free association of individual persons with others, all seeking their good in the group good. Ideally all forms of community offer help with problems, praise for success, and solace in failure. Since each member is accepted as an individual with particular talents and wants, each is responsible for his or her own status, role, and function. Conversely, because community helps to preserve the individual's freedom and transcendental hopes, members feel at home and can both maintain intimate convictions and express dissent without being ostracized (May 1933, 247–8). Thus community, by blending diversities in ways that all benefit, develops an easy working relationship among its members, which is one of the marks of true community.

Above all, community enriches the individual's personality. Drawing support from broad human themes—religious convictions, family feeling, school spirit, and neighborhood attachment—and by fostering people's natural habitat of fellowship, it provides a countervail against entrenched government and corporate power. The person experiences the kind of social ambience that makes it easier to posit higher values than merely satisfying material wants and desires. It goes beyond this, to being sensitive to what is right and due others and to being generous with time, talent, and money in helping others in need. Insofar as the sense of community is something of the mind and heart, its natural effect is to improve the way people live. Its values are social values and it says more about the spirit and intention of members than of the process and structure of the organization. In this way, it is especially beneficial for economic enterprise.

Community and the Gain Enterprise

The degree of community, of course, will vary significantly from one economic institution to another. In general, the smaller the unit size, the greater the possibility and intensity of community. In a small shop, office, or store, community can develop more readily with encouragement from the owner, since company goals are known to all. Also, in large economic enterprises the development of a feeling of community is more likely in its workshops, offices, or laboratories than in the company as a whole. Then, too, the nature and purpose of the business makes a difference: educational, cultural, health care, charitable, and similar services, to the extent their employees share their social values, will foster community more readily than commerce, manufacturing, or finance. Thus size and business climate may influence community's taking root, but the principal impediment to community in every kind of economic enterprise arises from *self-interested gain seeking*.

The desire for gain, as both appetite and economic drive, is as potent as the sex drive and as necessary. Indeed, increasing population requires an expanding and more productive economy. As major causes of conquests and interbreeding, these two drives are principal determinants of world demographics. Trying to keep the two in alignment and under control is not uniquely modern but as old and universal as humanity. In short and viewed separately, gain like sex, must be factored into most personal relationships, institutions, and communities. Money seeking, therefore, can be a source of conflict for any community, most seriously for families, kinships, and friendships, but also for religion, charity, or sports. Obviously, it is a greater and more endemic problem in economic institutions where gain seeking is both necessary and precarious.

Thus all economic associations are held together by balancing collaboration and sharing. For nonprofits this means servicing their constituents according to the social values the institution espouses and at the same time providing incomes to their workers and officers sufficient to support their families decently. In the same sense, profit-seeking businesses must balance productivity and profitability, each needing the other, since without profits productivity cannot be improved and without increased productivity profits languish. Thus the principle of *subsidiarity* really boils down to this: that participants in the economic process must be able to subsidize their personal and family welfare from their sharing in the material rewards that their collaboration earns.

For sure, fights over sharing are endemic in both profit-seeking and nonprofit institutions. But money and gain quarrels differ critically for manufacturing, retailing, finance, and businesses in general from personal, cultural, political, and similar groups. In nonprofit groups economic solvency and increasing capital are means to achieve the social ends and purposes of the institution and its community of committed persons. But for profit-seeking communities and institutions, gain and gain seeking are their very reasons for being.

That is, some participants in nonprofits can sacrifice for a time or even permanently give up some or any economic betterment for the sake of the higher values the community professes. But gain and profit are the very values that define profit-seeking companies. For sure, businesses may espouse human and even community values like friendliness, openness, and mutual contribution to and share in benefits. Even their hierarchic structures, by providing material ease and social status, may be much valued by their employees. Nevertheless, profits and gain, as the hopes of the combined efforts to produce goods and services, which have exchange value, are the paramount reasons why persons affiliate and stay with such organizations. No gain or profits, the business dissolves. That and the ubiquity of conflicts over gain, especially between labor and ownership, require examining gain seeking further.

ECONOMIC GAIN AND GROWTH

The emphasis here on gain and profits is needed to overcome the reluctance of many to accept their necessity. In fact, gain and profits labor under a like sense of shame that sex and sexual intercourse did generations ago. While open sex talk was taboo, it was practiced, as we are proof. No sex, no survival of the human race! Likewise, despite the qualms profits and gain may provoke, businesses survive by making profits, workers stay on the job because of gain, and customers return because they prefer products and services to money. Whatever sins are committed in the name of profits and gain, in light of the phenomenal growth of free-enterprise economies around the world, to deny the benefit they bring is quixotic. *Again, no gain or profits, no growth and no business!*

Economic science, therefore, must endorse maximizing gain as an analytic function in the logic of scarcity. Therefore, gain seeking is a *motive and prin-*

ciple of action in daily living. As consumers, laborers, entrepreneurs, or investors, people engage in economics always hoping to gain. The proof lies in the negative. A successful transaction may not elicit rejoicing but regret that the gain was less than expected. On the other hand, losses are universally deplored, unless less than anticipated, being a kind of negative gain. All, therefore, are telling witnesses of the intention to gain in every economic act.

To tell the truth that intention has paid off handsomely in the course of human history but never more spectacularly than in the last two centuries when free-market economic gain seeking became the rule in many nations. It vastly increased peoples' knowledge of themselves, of their minds and bodies, of their cultures and histories, of the universe they inhabit, of its resources, and dangers, and of other flora and fauna, past and present that Earth displays. People live much longer and have the knowledge and means to recover from illness and disabilities. They enjoy a larger, more reliable, and more varied food supply. Homes are more comfortable and better furnished to provide a greater range of activities. Distances between people and events have shrunk dramatically in time. Above all, people have come to expect that the pace of change will continue and, hopefully, accelerate.

All of this adds up to enormous increases in productive and consumption wealth. (That is, gain is the very increase in economic *weal*, or well-being which all wish to share.) This, more than accumulating marks, yens, and dollars or investment equivalents is the result of what was castigated as the infinite appetite for wealth. But it has its downside also. Gain seeking seems to promote a self-interested, if not a selfish, individualism that would seem to work against interpersonal cooperation, mutuality, and community in matters economic. The result is a dilemma! How can the spirit of gain seeking, which is necessary for both individual businesses and the entire economy to square with economic community, that bond which holds economic institutions together? Such suggests examining gain seeking from this social and communal aspect.

Gain as Social and Communal

Gain seeking seems to conflict with persons' social instincts and even more so with the spirit of community at three critical bastions of self-centered individualism. First, as unqualified seeking, that is, as a maximizing principle under conditions of scarcity, it would seem to put all the constituencies of the profit-seeking enterprise against each other; stockholders, workers, and managers among themselves; and suppliers and customers against them; each striving for the largest possible cut of the available pie. Second, as a self-interested principle it would seem to compound this competitive struggle by excluding the economic person's considerations of any other's well-being than one's own. Finally, as rationalized by the purely secular fact of economic scarcity, it would seem to preclude any meaning, value, or purpose beyond itself.

Individualistic gain maximizing, therefore, seems opposed to communitarian values, sharing, and mutual considerations, and the moral virtues restraining the gain appetite. All begs further examination.

First, maximizing, in implying no assignable limit, contradicts the very fact of economic scarcity. All economic goods and services, even what could be indefinitely increased, at any one moment are so much. Air, for an opposite example, while having a use value beyond all calculations, nevertheless, in being super abundant, has no exchange value for many of its uses but is free. Hence, to possess economic value a thing must be both limited and less than what is wanted or may be wanted. The gain motive, therefore, even though perhaps spurring production, sales, and profits, must also be finite and limited as it is realized in each economic act. *Unlimited gaining is self-defeating.*

Institutional gain is further controlled, since all economic acts involve some form of exchange. That is, each party freely surrenders what he or she values less for what is valued more. If, however, one consistently realizes a net gain while the other a net loss, exchange will eventually be impossible. In such a zero-sum game the loser will inevitably drop out. Marx saw the logic of this: the last capitalist exploiter/monopolist by acquiring everything destroys market capitalism. Maximizing gain, therefore, can only mean the best possible gains within internal and external limits, within constraints imposed by the market, technology, and resources. Keeping gain seeking within the limits of the possible alone meets the criteria of economic rationality. *Gain, in short, must not only be limited but shared.*

Even so, many assert that gain seeking as self-interested is radically individualistic self-seeking and thus a-social if not antisocial. This assertion, the second bulwark of individualism, however, ignores that the sale values of goods and services are what the market—that is buyers—will pay. However sellers can price monopolistically, their prices hold only if people want to buy. Selling needs buyers and something to sell, whose production, in turn, must be organized and financed. That is, the simplest economic act requires a chain of participants, all of whom become involved in the gain system whatever their roles.

Furthermore, economic efficiency requires that this blending of motives and abilities be done in the most advantageous manner. That is, every economic organization should use its personnel's diverse skills, know-how, and wealth in such manner as to exploit their respective *comparative advantages.* But specializing along one's comparative advantage creates advantages for others. The strong leave lighter jobs to weaker workers; the clever need the methodical; the skilled the unskilled; managers the managed; and the decision maker the decision performers. Consequently, to derive gain from an advantage mandates allowing others to gain from their advantages, however minimal they might be. Implicit in the rationality of self-interested gain seeking is enlisting others to cooperate toward a common purpose and respecting their desires, expectations, and needs in the sharing of a common good with them. That is, *complementarity and mutuality are intrinsic to gain seeking*. Thus the assumption that the gain motive is solely selfish also fades under the light of economic reality.

The third bastion of the gain drive relates to economics as a behavioral science with a strictly secular purpose. Economics treats only of the things and people in this universe and in the time of their lives. Like chemistry and physics, it deals with the here and now, but unlike them its agent is the economic person. That being's end and purpose in this life, therefore, define the values economics espouses: gain, money, wealth, price, and cost relate to using material things efficiently for living in this world. But all products and services with their related values are but means to the economic person's purposes as person.

Of the several personal goals, which readily come to mind, fame, physical prowess, pleasure, affluence, power, and the many kinds of human community all differ as possible and permanent. They may be pursued in sequence or in combination, but all except the last are flawed as lasting values. Pleasure and affluence can come and go; power and fame are necessarily limited to the few; physical prowess will inevitably ebb. But community and a sense of belonging as the natural product of innate social values like respect for personhood, love and friendship, and the desire for association can become anyone's permanent goals. The conclusion, therefore, is obvious. If economic success and gain can support the pursuit of purposes that are problematic, mutable, and transient, they can certainly serve as means to achieve goals like *community that relate to the economic person's nature and being*.

In summary, gain seeking has no rationale except to service human values and purposes, including not only vainglorious sensual values but also spiritual and, of especial concern here, communitarian. That economics is thought to serve only an egoistic materialism is not derived from economic rationality but from a philosophy of radical individualism, which equates economic agents' self-interest with selfishness, thus ignoring all the roles all people play as human persons, as embodied spirits. But since economic rationality is consistent with a personalist philosophy, it follows that personal moral habits are basic to guiding gain seeking toward economic community and thus fundamental for the healthy functioning of economic institutions.

THE MORAL BASES OF ECONOMIC COMMUNITY

Moral principles are basic to economic community, because economic agents are moral beings. Nevertheless, how economic and moral principles mesh in economic actions must always be stated carefully. Economic persons should strive to live virtuously in and for itself and not for economic gain. Conversely, bad economics does not foster virtue, the point being that virtue, while not without difficulties in practice, is consistent with good economics and should be of special concern for those who set the moral tone and establish the working philosophy for an economic institution. As for gain seeking, its wild spirit is a problem for community in the profit enterprise. An uncontrolled appetite for gain, with each seeking more for oneself at whatever cost to others and with no regard for fair sharing of burden and benefits, just destroys community. It implies a lust for gain that knows no bounds and little concern for others' rights and plights. The irrationality of such an attitude demands further examination of the gain drive and appetite in the light of virtuous living and specifically of moderation, justice, and a spirit of generosity.

Moderation

Moderation is not especially fashionable. The contemporary temper is to pursue with fervor and passion one's thing of the moment and, this paling, to take up something else. Indeed, some view moderation as lukewarm and temporizing, wanting in joy and spontaneity. But by braking the tendency to seek pleasures for oneself and, instead changing one's preferences toward goods of higher values and away from baser sensual values, moderation is simply the rationale of a person's fostering the right use of material goods. Moderation, by thus linking guiding and braking functions, achieves Aristotle's principle that all true virtues steer between excess and deficiency (Aristotle 1925, 1106b).

But the gain appetite presents particular problems. Unlike other sense appetites, whose objects are specific—this martini, this house—gain's objective is generic, money, or its surrogate, financial wealth. Since both promise and possess unlimited uses and use values, they, in fact, become ends in and for themselves. On the other hand, sense appetites, being specific, are subject to satiation and become addictions, cause physical harm. As such, they can be obnoxious to others and merit social ignominy. Gain suffers from neither affliction; successful gaining often whets the appetite for more, and its safekeeping is relatively easy. Finally, although the wealthy may be envied, even hated, they garner respect. Money trails a soothing, reverential aura, which earns not only others' regard but power over them. All in all, while the sense appetites seem to be more troublesome, the gain drive is more powerful, its growth more insidious, its vigor persisting when age and infirmity have abated the other appetites. Such is the Scholastic '*infinite appetite for riches*,' gain seeking run amuck, accumulating monetary, and financial wealth as ends in and for themselves.

Consequently, moralists have always warned of the gain appetite's propensity to cater to sensuality and to abet desires for precedence and power. Economists, on their side, have recognized that gain seeking, though energizing affluence, can work to the economy's detriment by corroding its essentially collaborative nature, by imperiling the environment, and by demanding more of the economy than it can produce.

Achieving community, therefore, would require dampening both consumerism and the all-out pursuit of profits without vitiating the gain motive itself. To managers, moderation urges growing in the business they know by improving product and workforce and by garnering consumer goodwill as surer ways to profits than moving into alien ventures, where profits are speciously enticing. To employees, it cautions holding wage demands within profitability and urges increasing that by improving productivity. To consumers, moderation warns that not all that neighbors have is worth their getting and that increasing one's income, while a healthy ambition, should not be pursued at the expense of personal growth, family welfare, community values, and friendships.

In the business enterprise, moderation will tend to encourage greater employee responsibility, more fellowship and pride in the product and thus customer satisfaction. But it will also prompt managers and owners to respect laborers' essential roles in all aspects of the economic enterprise and to reward accordingly. The effect is to help dissipate that climate of aggressiveness that makes community impossible, encouraging instead a spirit of cooperation that in the long run is more conducive to gain. Above all, moderating personal gaining permits sharing it more justly.

Justice

Indeed, just as moderation urges the right use of material things for self, justice directs their use for what is right for others. That justice is integral to economic conduct is obvious from calls for 'just wages and prices,' 'fair return on capital,' 'an honest day's work for a day's pay,' and so on. While most demands for justice seek to right an injustice to a plaintiff, justice does imply some objective standards of conduct. Its most basic precept is to respect others' rights, to treat everyone *rightfully*. Far from being egoistic, justice is basically a most social virtue and thus essential for economic community. It is especially requisite for *tempering the gain seeking* of everyone involved in the economic process and in economic institutions.

Essential to gaining is exchanging products or services for money and lending funds for a promise to repay with interest. Exchange, therefore, is a balancing act, each economic person preferring the other's property to one's own. Also, every exchange is but part of an endless concatenation of exchanges, past acts leading to present ones and current deals anticipating future exchanges, all being impacted by others' competitive buying and selling. Considering such complexities, libertarians espouse unregulated, individual trade as the most effective market system. Liberals, on the other hand, propose laws, even if forfeiting some benefits of free trade, to prevent the shrewd or callous from exploiting others' needs, ignorance, or disadvantages. But a sense of justice of most people and companies, who cherish a name for integrity, steers a middle way between a repressive legalism and a freedom tantamount to license. Despite the minority of swindlers of and predators on the poor and disadvantaged, the majority, if law-abiding, can be more effective in preserving economic freedom and thus fostering the integrity of the economic process itself.

This middle way in turn tends to steer a middle way through power policies. Too frequently, however, arguments for right order in profit-seeking businesses tend to swing from managerial authoritarianism to caving in to every union demand. This suggests that for them the real operating principle of such businesses is power, not justice, however much disputants mouth about fairness and their rights. But such destroys any possibility of real economic community, that is, true communal sharing.

It is further heightened by an impersonality which characterizes many business situations where people are processed like numbers and not as persons with roles to perform and aspirations to realize. Much of this is owing to anthropomorphizing the corporation as a legal person and as the agent of decisions and actions. But when for whatever reason the business fails, it is not the "corporation" that suffers but the people involved. All blurs the fact that a business is primarily and essentially a society of economic persons: managers, engineers, staff people, production workers, and maintenance crews related in a hierarchy of functions for the shared purpose of economic betterment through exchange.

When power supplants justice in internal disputes, another party suffers: the customer, who is the ultimate beneficiary of the larger economic community. Higher prices, shoddy goods, and poor service, all evidence of neglecting the customer, inevitably result from internal turmoil. Quality control, while good business in reducing waste and maintaining buyer goodwill, is really a form of justice to customers because guarantees, however well honored, never fully recompense customer frustrations, loss of time, and use of property. A sense that people and their wants are important, whether within or outside a business, is a fundamental prescription of economic justice. As such it is a basic requirement of community and of every economic institution.

Because people associate in an economic enterprise only to better their economic condition—to gain—income distribution is the acid test for affirming respect for persons. While customer sales adequate to recompense costs of production are the main source of gain in free markets, and while the liberty to buy/sell, hire/work, lend/borrow, and the rest is the most efficient system for a highly productive economy and a rapidly changing society, freedom to gain cannot in and of itself achieve justice in the distribution of gain. Justice here involves other nuances.

A sense of justice, finally, must realize that the multidimensional business relationship makes gauging precisely a just determination of compensation, profits, and prices impossible. But such a stance will accept everyone's *right to gain*, will engage a spirit of compromise in the face of scarcity, will admit past failures and be willing to rectify them, and will evince a dogged resolve to keep the operation going as the *common good of all*. It will keep its cool in controversy, especially aware of gain seeking's tendency to excess but all the while insisting that the business must be profitable, that workers want more income and customers better products. Called 'square shooting,' 'giving a fair shake,' 'making reasonable demands,' or whatever, a *many-faceted justice must be in play in a gain-seeking enterprise*.

Such sensitivity to others' rights, when broadly shared by economic persons in the organization, will mitigate much dissent and generate a set of principles by which conflicts can be reasonably compromised. Seen in this light, justice is not a harpy, swooping down upon every misdeed and miscue, but a solvent of disagreements and a promoter of community. Justice, moreover, is basic and prelude to a spirit of generosity about one's material goods.

A Spirit of Generosity

Beyond moderation in pursuing wealth and a just sharing with its coproducers, a true understanding of gain sees it not as an end in itself but as means to fulfill life's purpose. A spirit of community, furthermore, goes beyond personal wants to include the needs of the truly poor. A spirit of generosity thus epitomizes the rationality and justice of economic personalism by preferring another's needs over one's pleasures, justice requiring that one subsidize another's right to survive in preference to one's own right to comforts and conveniences.

The religious *spirit of poverty* has for millennia inspired men and women to share their wealth with others for love of them as children of God (Danner

1994, 165–90), but even a secular version, inspired by fellow feeling for human suffering, has power to urge the well-off to help those in need. In so doing generous spirits demonstrate they know the end and purpose of wealth and how it fits easily into community, even in businesses organized to generate gain and wealth.

A generous person, while appreciating wealth, is always willing to share his or her well-being by feeding the poor, providing schools and health programs, making peace, and rehabilitating the victims of misfortune. A generous spirit is as creative and all-embracing as life, perceiving even in affluence new ways of helping not only the poor but the alcoholic, the drug addict, the battered, and the sexually abused, all who are physically or psychologically crippled for modern living. Such postures will help unite people and will find use for even those who have no use for themselves. Paradoxically, this will generate more wealth by salvaging the savable than it will dissipate in maintaining the totally irresponsible.

Unlike much current wisdom that suspects that wealth is in and of itself demoralizing and gain is divisive, a generous spirit sees wealth as the unfolding of nature's bounty. In cooperative ventures it counsels not becoming morose over hard bargains but being appreciative of earning goodwill, if not money. It offers balm for the nagging thoughts of others' successes and one's own failures. It is a source of strength in the trauma of change: a disability requiring vocational reorientation, a new boss with different demands, or events beyond one's control causing unemployment or termination. Finally, it is a salve when called to give beyond duty, when events require one to bear a burden for which one is not responsible, assuming the role and duty of what moral theologians call the Suffering Servant.

All this is good for community: a generous spirit eases the inevitable conflicts and is sensitive to others' needs even at the expense of one's wants. Above all, a sense of generosity gives ultimate meaning to gain seeking, proposing as its basic reason those deep human and shared values fostered by community: personal growth in a cooperative enterprise, providing products and services to others, family well-being, good citizenship, and concern for those needing help, all of which are important for the functioning of economic institutions.

Thus generosity plus moderation and justice is totally integrating. They unite self-seekers toward a common goal and spread an easing oil at all the abrasive points of human interaction in the workplace, in giving and obeying orders, in admonishing and encouraging, and in preserving personal aims within the general interest. These virtues also integrate economic goals with overall life purposes, not only by motivating work effort with significant purpose but by thereby making one's job an important part of living itself. Finally, they mitigate the work frustrations, often spewed out in private life, and can assuage private grief by support from fellow employees. Community is no panacea for all the problems of business, but it will make the individual's life more personal, more social, and more livable.

Community, of course, cannot be imposed by fiat nor can the virtues foundational to community be commanded into being. Such a program demands continuous effort by all and particularly some moral leadership preferably from the CEO and the management team. But such high-mindedness is not prerequisite. Managers can move to the high ground by means of hardheaded analysts of gain and the conviction that persons make the economy go.

Economics was always understood as a factor in the equation for human living, first as relating to principles for managing a household, then as its principles were applied to the economic functions of nation-states, and now to the global economy. Inevitably, as their scope widened, economic principles were more and more universalized and mathematicized. Pertinent here, gain seeking was seen to be the universal drive of economic action. But its agents are human persons who have careers, vocations, and destinies, which relate all to all, not only physically but politically, culturally, and economically. Briefly put, persons naturally seek community even in their economic life. Put another way: every person is in a real sense an economic person.

Just as community is essential for every economic institution and every association with an economic element—in short, for every human relationship—it becomes an essential element of the societal and political Common Good.

REFERENCES

Aristotle. *Nichomachean Ethics*. Translated by W. D. Ross. Oxford: Clarendon, 1925.

Boswell, Jonathan. *Community and the Economy: The Theory of Public Co-operation*. New York: Routledge, 1990.

Danner, Peter L. *Getting and Spending: A Primer in Economic Morality*. Kansas City, Mo.: Sheed and Ward, 1994.

——. "The Moral Foundations of Community." *Review of Social Economy* 42, no. 3, 1984: 231.

Gelin, Albert. *Les Pauvres de Yahve*. Paris: Les Editions du Cerf, 1955.

May, Rollo. *Power and Innocence: A Search for the Sources of Violence*. New York: Norton, 1933.

Nisbet, Robert A. *Community and Power*. New York: Galaxy, 1962.

Noonan, John T. Jr. *The Scholastic Analysis of Usury*. Cambridge, Mass.: Harvard University Press, 1957.

Smith, Adam. *An Inquiry into the Nature and Causes of the Wealth of Nations*. Edited by Edward Cannan. New York: The Modern Library, 1937.1

Chapter Nine

Personalism and Common Good

Even though economic science has become more quantitative in its theorizing and more mechanistic in ascribing causation to governments, markets, unions, corporations, and such, still persons as consumers, workers, managers, investors, and taxpayers are the ultimate economic agents. Persons, as embodied spirits, must, to survive as a species, transform the resources and powers of the material universe into useful goods and services. This in turn requires a comprehensive price system and the universal desire to gain, to improve one's economic condition, by designing better ways of producing products others want.

No less as spiritual and moral beings, persons who need to relate to and communicate with other persons, to implement their striving for truth and beauty, and to achieve moral values, require producing and exchanging goods and services bearing economic values. In other words, persons' economic dealings with others are essential to knowing both others and themselves. Thus persons are not only necessary agents of the economic process, but that process and the institutions and communities it creates are essential elements for both those persons' own well-being and for the Common Good, here meaning all the social bonds relating persons in the various social, political, and economic roles each performs.

SOCIETY, POLITY, AND ECONOMY

Obviously persons enact their individual dramas in different settings and play many roles in relation to others, such as spouses, children, friends, coworkers, and fellow citizens. While people have difficulty meeting the demands their roles impose, most can manage the minimum requirements of the social

131

web in which they are enmeshed. In so doing they lay the foundation of comity and mutual help, required for the Common Good. Analysis, therefore, must begin with people's social needs, their relationships with each other and the roles their need and relations require them to play. In short, it demands examining the social, political, and economic Common Good.

Social Needs, Relations, and Rules

Persons' social needs are as essential as their survival needs. They cannot begin to exist, survive, or develop their humanity except as related to other persons in a tridimensional web of personal, political, and economic relations. Of personal bonds, gender ties can create the most basic needs, like spouses' needs for intimacy and children's needs for bonding, nurture, and guidance. Cultural needs are most comprehensive and varied, like the need for civility and fellowship and the need to share ideas, feelings, hopes, and fun with kinfolk and friends. Authors, artists, and actors need audiences. Students require masters and mentors, professional and practical. All must trust experts for medical and legal aid, media people for the news, and scholars to preserve and organize civilization's accumulated knowledge and to separate the trivial from treasures in the daily flow of ideas, letters, and art. The poor and disadvantaged depend upon others' know-how and charity to gain access to the mainstream and sometimes just to survive.

Besides these mainly personal relations, persons are bound to each other politically and economically. They relate politically, like senator to constituents, to establish, and maintain public peace and order, and economically, like buyers to sellers, to achieve efficiency in producing, exchanging, distributing, and using scarce material goods. Conversely, practically every social bond between and among persons, even that between mother and baby, is of some concern to the state and certainly needs economic support to survive.

Similarly, economic, and business dealings have their civil and political side because they pertain to public order. For the economy to function, property, and property rights must be protected, dangers reduced, markets kept orderly, and credit and money trustworthy. On the other hand, the political order draws heavily from the economic for the resources to keep its vast and complex operations going. While these relations can be considered separately, they never in fact work in isolation. Disturbances in the political order affect the most private ties. Events in the economy impact on political and personal well-being. Changes in personal relations—marriages and divorces, births and deaths, feuds and fellowships—are the very stuff of politics and economics.

The dimensions of these relations are usually, but not necessarily, complementary and corroboratory. Personal ties flourish better in a peaceful, law-abiding public arena than in a crime infested one and in a modestly flourishing economy than in a depressed one. The economy prospers when personal and factional disputes are minimal. Political order thrives when people know, respect, and get along with each other. On the other hand, family ties can accentuate crime, business nepotism can sap profitability, corporate practice can harm neighborhoods, and government policy can break up families. In short, people are so linked personally, politically, and economically that anything occurring in one forum ramifies into the others.

As consequence, every person plays many more roles than Shakespeare's seven and plays these simultaneously. A woman might be wife, mother, sister, neighbor, boutique manager, chairperson of the mission society, and more, all at the same time. These roles relate her to others and together involve her in a complex of priorities, interdependencies, and obligations. How people play their roles, form social relations, and espouse values relative to them in daily intercourse is infinitely varied and can only be suggested here. Specific, however, to this study, the social values of liberty, equality, and fraternity most importantly influence how persons act as members of society, as citizens of the polity, and as economic agents and thus, how they relate to each other personally, politically, and economically.

Society

Primarily each person is related to every other, everywhere and forever. These ties are intrinsically natural, essential, and inclusive. All, therefore, belong to society by birth. None can be excluded entirely, either by chance, personal choice, or public banishment. Consequently, this encompassing web of personal ties, including family and kinship ties along with all forms of cultural sharing—school, church, neighborhood, workplace, and artistic and civic assemblies—enjoys the highest priority as essential for human generation, survival, and growth into fully developed and mature persons. Since everyone is validly and equally human, society remains healthy as long as individual, gender, and ethnic differences are both tolerated and integrated into the cultural mainstream. Respect for each's duties and rights as well as free association and communication are essential for a healthy society.

While society commands priority over polity and economy (both of whose relations are necessarily social) society still needs both political peace and order as well as a well functioning economy. A licentious and lawless society not only breeds enmities, hatreds, and crimes but also frustrates those social and cultural institutions which enhance human living. An indulgent society dissipates its resources, encourages greed and envy, and denigrates work and saving. On the other hand, an ossified and rigidly structured economy destroys initiative, because the powerful rich are content with the status quo and the masses too cowed to challenge it. Finally, society flourishes best with a modest prosperity as does the polity.

Polity

The polity consists of those relationships by which a people constitute themselves formally or de facto as a corporate body with a government empowered to maintain peace and order, that is, to become a state. While the polity, or state, is entirely natural, it is not inherent in personhood. Membership in the state can be limited, revoked, or denied and, conversely, a person can leave a state and renounce citizenship. Thus the state is *subsidiary* to society and economy and it should not appropriate functions which individuals or private groups can do for themselves.

The polity is also vested with power to set and enforce laws to maintain peace and order. Public peace helps people to go about their business and to engage in the community's social and cultural life with minimum exasperation or danger. In modern states the task of preserving peace and order multiplies into a complex of institutions with powers, ranging from national defense to protecting endangered species (not excluding humankind). At times civic disorder may require some intolerance or diversity and deviant behavior, allow intrusion into intimate matters, and justify some interfering in private business.

Obviously, the state needs the power to protect property, to enforce contracts, and to safeguard the economic process. It means having the right to define, to render, and to enforce justice by restraining such business activity that harms the common good, takes advantage of employees, or defrauds customers. At the same time, the state requires a prospering economy, needing its productivity to fund its multifarious functions. An oppressive state, by laying on burdensome taxes, cramping business with restrictive laws, and intervening in otherwise orderly free markets, can harm the very economy upon which it depends for survival.

Statism and totalitarianism are, consequently, the normal result of unchecked political authority, which dislikes the autonomy of free markets so that it is constantly tempted to substitute its laws for moral principles, its controls for business skill, and its welfarism for personal responsibility. Unchecked, it inevitably creates privileged castes who increasingly rule for their own good at the expense of the general public. The antidote is an *open society*, where everyone is in fact equal before the law, diversity is safeguarded, minority rights are protected, and all can participate in the public forum. Above all its governors should be periodically reviewed by the governed and its people mainly free to seek their economic well-being as they see fit.

Economy

While the economy, with its buildings, factories, machines, farms, fleets, and forests, appears to be, more so than polity or society, a physical thing, it is primarily a vast network of all economic persons related to each other in conceiving, producing, and distributing goods and services throughout the world. As such it is coterminous with society, and equally natural, inherent and necessary. Economic activity arises spontaneously from the facts of limited but differently possessed natural resources and limited but differently endowed human skills and material resources. It can be as complex as a transnational company producing and selling globally or as simple as selling rights to whitewash a fence.

Since persons associate economically to provide the material means for living, these relations are subsidiary to both society and polity. They are, however, derived from neither but from the basic facts that embodied spirits need material goods to survive and to act and must, therefore, cooperate to obtain them. While persons must take different roles as managers, workers, consumers, investors, or whatever, all require two components: collaboration and competition. Together they generate the natural and spontaneous economic drive of *self-interested gain seeking*.

Economic production without any collaboration with others, for sure, is most rare, and exchanging without correspondents is impossible. The result is a distinctive kind of self-interested gain seeking in which persons succeed by sharing and exploit advantage by proffering something more or better. The seller gains by tendering better products or cutting price; the buyer by paying more. The successful boss gets better work by paying higher wages; the willing employee by working for less or more diligently. In sum, collaboration, competition, and thus *self-interested gain seeking* are inherently social.

Since society and polity depend on the economy for survival, social and political leaders must respect the principles and methodology by which workshops operate, offices run, banking and finance function, and free markets behave. In turn, economists must accept persons as they are, differing in interests, abilities, and ambitions, each with his or her particular personal relations and roles to play, but each necessarily participating in the economy as self-interested gain seekers.

Likewise, while politics and business may from time to time be adversarial, both need each other: the state needs a prospering economy to support its programs and activities, and the economy needs the state's legal structure and public services to do business. The economy is helped even more by laws restraining selfish self-interest, which, by undermining collaboration, impairs the economic process itself. More positively, any government or private program that increases people's competence and skills, improves their quality of life, or enhances their dignity cannot be bad for the economy or for business. Given right attitudes, harmonizing the respective functions of society, polity, and economy is not only possible but in everyone's best interest.

While political, moral, and social leaders may dispute for turf among themselves and those with most prestige, influence, and power affect public policy to their liking, in an open and democratic society the mass of inconsequential persons carries the most weight. The concerns they feel, the issues which affect their lives, and their instincts as to what constitutes the good life will ultimately determine the configuration of public order. Persons eventually get what their feelings and instincts dictate, and these in turn are largely governed by the *values*, be they noble or base, sensual or spiritual, which they espouse.

SOCIAL VALUES AND THE PUBLIC ORDER

Values are not simply feelings, though perhaps deeply felt. They are imbedded convictions, "deeply propriate disposition(s)" upon which "a man acts by preference" (Allport 1965, 126 and 454). They are filters through which a person sees and understands reality. "A value is characterized by its depth, by the extent it brings order to experience" (Scruton 1979, 32). The Common Good, therefore, as a social dynamic is best understood by analyzing the social values which foster it.

Values and Social Values

To recall the earlier Schelerian analysis: a value is an immediate perception (intuition) of a good, one's own, another's, a thing's, or of a relation among persons or things, its good ranked according to its essence, duration, unity, and wholeness. Scheler then includes all experiences of good, from the ephemeral pleasure of a chocolate bar to a radically transforming experience as a value event (Vide: chapter 6, 86-90).

Social values, however, are values espoused by many people but by each in a distinct form. Patriotism, or love of country, for example, is a value widely cherished by many but in unique ways: some are willing to sacrifice life for it, others to protest injustice by disobeying laws. Such variations aside, personal convictions are not only confirmed but hardened by harmonizing one's relations and dealings with others. National events like a wanton attack can spark latent social values which charismatic leaders, in turn, can fan into national movements, generating powerful forces for changing both the social and public order.

Of many social values *freedom*, *equality*, and *fraternity* are the best known and most rooted in Western thinking and culture. (Some prefer community to fraternity. But here community relates more to specific groups, whereas fraternity is inclusive of all citizens of a given state.) The three values can be found at the fountainhead of Mediterranean civilization. Achilles's tragedy evolves around his freedom as a warrior, his assertion of equality with Agamemnon, and his love for Patroclus. Christian belief carries these to a higher dimension in belief that Christ freed mankind from sin and Satan's power, that all are equally loved by the Creator, and that as children of God all are Christ's brothers and sisters.

Manifested as a political creed, the three social values were formulated in the Enlightenment and given concrete expression in the Declaration of Independence, when thirteen contentious colonies united to assert "that all men are created equal; that they are endowed by their Creator with certain inalienable rights; that among these are life, liberty, and the pursuit of happiness." (This last is best attained by social beings in devotion to, love for, and in community with other persons.) "Liberty, Equality, Fraternity!" became the rallying cry of the French Revolution and inspired the Declaration of the Rights of Man and the Citizen. Since then every constitution of states choosing a democratic form of government has echoed this triad of social values.

But accepting these values as ideals is not to realize them in practice. The great American dilemma has been the difficulty of granting effective civil liberty to the descendants of former African slaves (Myrdal 1944). A less disquieting but persistent problem is the quandary of welcoming the world's poor and disenfranchised with the difficulty of assimilating them into the cultural mainstream. That the United States is still a rainbow of peoples and cultures is owing to the efficacy, while not perfect, of freedom and equality. That it is not a totally united people testifies to the relative weakness of community/fraternity. Since all social values are rooted in human personhood, their failures or effectiveness gauge the state of social, political, and economic intercourse and the quality of public life. It becomes necessary to see how they complement and conflict with each other.

Liberty and Personal Freedom

Liberty and freedom are often used synonymously. But each features one of the two essential notes of the reality: liberty, exemption from restraint, and freedom, the right to seek one's good. Since the human person is subject to differing layers of restraint—from the very physical to the highly spiritual—and may seek many categories of good, human liberty/freedom differs from person to person and changes with life's circumstances.

Time and space limit movement; the need for provision, rest, air, and so forth restrict efforts and activities; procreative acts require a partner; sensory deficiencies impair perceptions and sensations; imaginations are conditioned by past experiences and the capacity for enjoyment by cultivation; thoughts, and hopes require words, numbers, and other means of expression. The good that people seek also ranges from the mainly material and physical to the spiritual, like learning, reasoning, willing, and so to the heart's ineffable aspirations. Relations among persons also vary in the respect owing them. Most sacred are family ties: spouses' vows, parent/child/sibling bonds, and other blood relationships. Freedom to form friendships must be protected as must the vast array of cultural, professional, and educational ties people form. Even casual contacts deserve respect. In sum, personal freedom, whatever constraints, relations, and aspirations are relevant, underlies each person's right to seek the good and to grow into one's true self.

Political freedom for all adult, nonimprisoned citizens, as evidenced in freedom of religion, speech, assembly, and press and the rights to vote, to stand for office, to protection of person and property, and to a fair and public trial is the real blessing of modern democracies. Economic freedom, however, is more chancy in its beneficence. Even though sociopolitical freedom requires generally free markets, private property, open competition, and the rights to hire and be hired, nonetheless economic wealth is unequally distributed and shared. Some people have more market power, own more property, enjoy greater competitive advantage, and can put more people to work for them. In short, economic freedom produces great inequalities (and also inequities) and it is here that liberty and equality as social values most sharply conflict.

Equality and Individuality

Addressing this conflict requires first laying out the basic dichotomy in the idea of equality itself. Essentially all people are equally person: in some sense self-aware, responsible, social, and transcendent. At the same time each person is an individual, uniquely existing here and now, differentiated from every other actual or possible human being in age, size, experience, talent, and biology. To be completely human one must be fully personal and uniquely individual. Equality, therefore, requires respecting everyone as a person, while treating each differently as an individual. It requires discerning when equal treatment violates persons' individuality and when treating individuals differently violates their sense of equality as persons.

As members of society, all individuals must be respected as persons with rights to fulfill their physical, vital, social, and spiritual needs, each in a singular way, the disadvantaged being accorded special help. As citizens, all are equal before the law, even though taxed differentially by wealth and income. Likewise, while people generally accept that the poor should be protected and helped economically, all tend to agree that in economic transactions no one should be preferred or discriminated against on the basis of noneconomic criteria: race, gender, politics, and so on.

In fact, therefore, freedom to be different precludes identical treatment. Only the few achieve fame, and honor; most live and die in obscurity. Some gain respect and affection; others are lonesome and ignored. The rich and the well organized have more political power than the poor and disorganized. Incumbents enjoy advantages over challengers. The wealthy can afford more costly litigation, while the poor are more subject to military service and ex-convicts more suspected of crimes. Economic freedom means the wealthy, talented, shrewd, and ambitious, not to say the dishonest and unscrupulous, can garner property, capital, and power much above the average. All these disparate effects of equality and liberty argue for a third social value mediating them.

Fraternity and Solidarity

Of the three values, fraternity is the least appreciated and the most needed. Clarence Walton is quite blunt: "To dwell on notions of justice, liberty, and fraternity is to recognize how much and how long Western man has talked of the first, more recently of the second, and almost never of the third. . . . Indeed it is quite possible that contemporary liberal political thought which supports egalitarianism is essentially individualistic and unfraternal" (Walton 1977, 28).

The *value-fraternity* consists in seeing one's social nature not just as linkages to others but as alliances that complement one's limitations. Fraternity, therefore, can permeate all one's relations to others, the most necessary to the most incidental. Fraternity engenders community, that sense of being accepted as a member of a group, of being one with others, of belonging. It is called *solidarity* because it solidifies the differing talents and interest of people into common goals or purposes. Hence it respects their personalities while accepting their uniqueness and individuality. By creating unity from diversity, fraternity affirms the equal right of all to contribute to and to share in the Common Good but in a way specific to each. Fraternity safeguards human personality by respecting both one's individuality and relations to others.

The Social Triad in Action

But the value roles of fraternity, liberty, and equality are not set once for all but are in constant process as persons' apprehensions, aspirations, and moral concerns change. They not only relate as social values and respond to how others think and act but, by guiding action they establish consistency in behavior and eventually form habits—hopefully virtues but unfortunately also vices. Thus immoderate liberty begets selfishness in dealing with others, degrades many personal bonds into cash connections, and induces the worst business license. Conversely, when political privilege dominates the economy and economic conduct, uncurbed bureaucrats can transform its welfare systems into patronage. When people become more concerned about equality of rights, fraternal feelings disappear and society is polarized, envy inciting the poor against others' privileges and the wealthy hoarding those same advantages. Then, too, a spurious fraternity can beget a tribalism or clannishness which renders the state impotent and the economy stagnate. Conversely, a sham solidarity creates an all-powerful, ruling elite, who with their minions dominates society for their own advantage.

When, however, people espouse these social values in a balanced way, a general accord will prevail among personal attitudes, ordinary social intercourse, business practice, and public policy. A fundamental accord may prevail despite differences and disputes, just as sibling squabbling may cover up a basic comity. So too, the Common Good will manifest certain unifying features: respect for each and all as free and responsible persons; tolerance, even indulgence, of diversity; acceptance of everyone, especially of the poor and dispossessed, as equally human; a common obligation to contribute to and having the right to share in the public good; and a sense of community as an overall social harmonizer. In short, all are respected both as persons and as individuals and all belong, blending their contributions into the common life.

But with this multifaceted dynamic, complacency is never in order. All must guard against the hateful word and act. Social arbiters, political leaders, moral critics, public commentators, and others while, it is hoped, possessing a sense of social balance themselves, must be alert to maintain the symmetry and proportions among the personal, political, and economic facets of public life.

While the preceding analysis can be applied to both society and polity, this chapter is limited to showing how it relates to the economic person and bears upon the social economy. There the same triad of social values, which keep society, polity, and economy working together, will be shown to orientate and coordinate the principles which ideally motivate the economic person, as differentiated from the *homo economicus* of economic analysis, and make the economy function.

THE ECONOMY AND SOCIAL VALUES

The economy, as a complex of economic persons who produce goods and services, distribute income and profits, trade output for money, consume their collective production, or invest savings in new technologies or to service future wants, is a social aggregate and a vast liturgy. Its components include all kinds of productive means—buildings, machines, equipment, and inventory, for example—but mainly people organized into office forces, marketing staffs, production crews, and management teams in factories, financial houses, service centers, shopping malls, government bureaus, and nonprofit agencies, serving the needs of persons, families, schools, churches, charities, governments, and other businesses.

What makes this vast, complex, and seething organism function are its three principles of organization: competitive gain seeking, government mediation, and cooperative collaboration. *Competitive gain seeking* is the drive and impelling force; *government involvement* is the safeguard, the guiding but mainly braking action; *cooperation* is fundamental for the economic process to function at all. The three social values which harmonize economic persons' social, political, and economic relations do double duty in keeping the economy's organization principles in order. Freedom spurs competition; equality sanctions political mediation; fraternity fosters cooperation. Each principle will be discussed in turn.

Competitive Gain Seeking

Gain seeking is the economy's most basic principle of organization: needing and wanting material goods makes the economy go. Some things like air and light are there for the taking, but most must be produced. Because all human material wants at any time exceed what is currently available, people must either use what is on hand more efficiently, by shifting, trading, or redesigning things from less to more desired uses, or make more of the same. In other words, the very nature of the human condition mandates that economic persons be free to better their material being—*to gain*. Since all experience some economic stringency, they must be free to compete for everything they own or use. This may be judged antagonistic by overly "aesthetic" moralists, but for economic persons as embodied spirits it is the only way to survive and to grow. It lays out the path of human progress from caves to suburbia. In sum, the essential principle driving the economy is free, *competitive gain seeking*.

For sure, competitive gain seeking is self-interested, but as economic it differs from other forms of competition. Most such are adversarial, that is, winners get prizes, losers get nothing. Worse, betting winners gain what losers lose. And worst, a thief, netting in his risks and costs, gains less than what his victim loses, for a net social loss. On the other hand, altruism is generally socially profitable, the indigent benefitting more from what the charitable lose by giving. Competitive gain seeking falls between in being mutually, though perhaps not equally, beneficial. One gains by offering more at lower prices than competitors, who, nevertheless, still have product to sell. The reverse, of course, is true for buyers: those offering more buy while the losers have money to try again. Winners gain but losers are no worse off. *Economic self-interest*, therefore, not only implements the basic rationality of getting the most return from effort and resources, but it is *essentially social*.

Consequently, competitive gain seeking, since it is designed to better one's economic lot by striving for efficiency, is *self-interested but not necessarily selfish*. That is, it abstracts from persons' reasons or purposes for acting, simply affirming that competitors should seek to increase their economic gain, whether they alone benefit, or others, or both. Thus competitive gain seeking, as an economic principle, relates to economic efficiency, not to moral purpose, whether that is selfish or altruistic. Soup kitchen volunteers must be as concerned for efficiency in serving all their guests as the supermarket manager for profits. (Maybe more so, since their purpose is nobler!) It defies common sense to ascribe all economic motives to selfishness rather than to admit the commonsense fact that people act economically for greatly varied and often mixed moral and personal reasons. Nevertheless, whatever the purpose, rationality requires *efficient use*.

Thus real-life competition, as gain seeking's spur, must also be distinguished from the pale, mechanistic abstraction of economic, especially neo-Classical, analysis. Bernard W. Dempsey was a generation ahead of most contemporaries in perceiving real-life competition as a *constructive, vigorous, and innovative* force even among huge commercial, financial, and manufacturing enterprises. "American competition is a new thing in economics. It is itself an undigested innovation. It is not atomistic; it does not deal with small units. It is not impersonal: innovations come from persons; only people, not markets, have ideas" (Dempsey 1958, 336). Only lately have political economists begun to acknowledge openly the benefits of competition even in such hallowed enterprises as the education of children. But being as aggressive as it is, competitive gain seeking can easily turn to selfish and greedy ends. Hence it needs some controls.

Government Mediation

The polity as guardian of the Common Good can set the parameters within which the economy functions: civil order, justice, a trustworthy money, and so forth. The government's duty and appropriate role to exercise prudent oversight respecting the public welfare can be "described in four functions: directing, watching, urging, and restraining" (Dempsey 1958, 283). Thus dictating regulations is likely to be less beneficial and even more harmful than the business policies and ethos a company may formulate on its own.

But government must, above all, protect the right of all to be treated equally as persons, while differentially treated as individuals. There is both a positive and negative side to such government intervention in economic matters. The negative would imply laws and their enforcement against stealing, arson, fraud, extortion, libel, perjury, and all grasping for advantage by the powerful and/or unscrupulous against the poor and/or law-abiding. The positive first and foremost requires protecting persons and property, both public and private, and administering justice. It further suggests subsidizing education and public health, relieving catastrophic losses, supplementing the income of the poor, sustaining the hungry, homeless, and unemployed, taxing differentially, and whatever seems necessary to alleviate disadvantage.

The benefit, at times the need, of some state engagement in the economy is too obvious to dispute. Restraining evil acts and promoting honest dealing improve the climate of personal trust essential for business. Programs that enhance economic persons' earning capacity, create new jobs, or renew hope after disasters increase the productivity of the economy. There will always be the disadvantaged, physically, culturally, or through personal fault. Unfortunately children will be included among them. Every effort, personal, communal, and governmental, therefore, which rescues families and persons from submerging permanently into the underclass makes a positive contribution to the economy.

Conversely, policies, and programs that penalize self-interest (as distinct from guiding it), that favor monopoly over reasonable competition, that tend to patronize people and to lock them into dependency, violate the economy's operating principles and *do more harm than good.*

Cooperation and Collaboration

While competitive gain seeking drives the economy and state action guides it, *cooperative collaboration* is its operational mode (Dempsey 1958). "Cooperation in the economic process is both implicit and explicit." People and property "working together on a job are obviously cooperating." But in expecting to exchange their output for what others produce, they are "also cooperating toward a common objective, namely the provision of an improved standard of living for both" (Dempsey 1958, 21 and 23). The need for cooperative collaboration flows from the basic reason for private property and, even more, from the specialization of labor. Further since neither work nor property is productive by itself, further product development requires even more diversified and higher skills, more refined resources, and more complex collaboration.

Collaboration performs a further function in linking state involvement with competition. It effects the same purpose as government's. When a larger population works at and shares in a greater economic output, more income and wealth are generated and spread more widely. At the same time cooperation preserves, indeed encourages, gain seeking. By improving productivity, it heightens competition among firms. By offering more income, it spurs persons to greater effort in their jobs. In sum, economic collaboration arises from the human person's material wants and needs as an embodied spirit and in cooperation with others as a social being. But like all things human, nothing comes easy and without a struggle.

The Principles in Conflict

While the economic organizing principles in theory engender harmony, the spasmodic or excessive emphasis on one to the harm of the others provokes discord. Unprincipled gain seeking tends to dissolve the social ties which make the economy a Common Good. Selfish aggrandizement, particularly — but not only—by owners and managers, sours cooperation into coercion. A crude and selfish self-interest reduces workers to means and buyers or sellers to things to be exploited. More subtle selfishness will sire intimidation and deception, masked as vigorous competition. Such attitudes breed that alienation that Marx claims is intrinsic to capitalism, subverting both the workshop and marketplace into cockpits of contending atomistic individuals (Marx 1952, chs. 7 and 25).

The political reaction to selfish self-interest is some form of egalitarianism, which in taking the value equality to extremes intrudes into the economy in a damaging way. Ideological egalitarianism inevitably generates a governing elite, whose economic and political privileges camouflage a selfish class-interest: *the pigs are more equal than the rest*! A more pragmatic egalitarianism, often motivated by sincere desires to provide needed assistance, to redress disadvantage, or to secure the public from devious practices, tends, like the proverbial camel, to take over the economy. Laws supposedly clear-cut and written to apply to specific situations, inevitably are reinterpreted to fit changed circumstances in ways which might proscribe what the original legislation never intended, or to prescribe its opposite.

The basic difficulty is that legal relations are relatively fixed, while economic relations in response to gain seeking, competition, and collaboration are constantly changing. Thus state subsidies and entitlements, while intended to provide necessary assistance, tend to breed dependency first among the poor. Then it infects the middle classes and becomes blatant with a corporate welfarism more addictive than the dole. All of this will inevitably discriminate against private programs, which provide the same services. It illustrates again that generally governments are not comfortable with competition, preferring legally set prices to market prices, regulation to capricious economic rivalry, and franchised monopolies to having many vying for the same business.

Finally, a cooperation, infected by complacency, collusion, or both, does not, despite appearances, resolve the competition versus intervention conflict. Rather, it skirts around it or covers it up. The complacent disdain competition, being superior to it and satisfied with the status quo (Detroit's attitude to the upstart Japanese competition during the 1950s.). A smug management and contented labor force will make common cause in seeking government protection especially from foreign competition. Other kinds of collusion—rigged bids, sweetheart contracts between owners and union, insider trading and dealing, imitative pricing—may actually be illegal or cut corners. In short, complacency and collusion tend both to defuse competition and to blunt government intervention with the result not only of slowing the economy but, worse, unraveling its social ties.

But just as the same people, who act as economic consumers, competitors, and collaborators in the social economy interact as social persons, political citizens, and economic agents, so the social values of *liberty*, *equality*, and *fraternity* can facilitate coordinating the social economy's three organizing principles.

Values and Principles in Concert

Liberty inspires respect for everyone as a person, whether engaged in social intercourse, business activity, or public policy. It defends those rights essential to an effective competition, the overall right to participate in the economy, including benefitting from economic opportunity, engaging in competition, and exploiting one's skills and advantages. Liberty accepts the basic rightness that those whose effort, ideas, risk-taking, and skill generated a larger return should benefit from their actions. Liberty would extend all of these rights as widely as possible and defend them vigorously. As to public policy it prefers private initiative to government undertaking and the market process to political fiat. In short, the state does not dominate but is *subsidiary* to the economy.

Equality, on the other hand, does welcome some government involvement and intervention as not only needed at times but also beneficial. In recognizing everyone's right to share in the economy's output, equality supports laws and courts in suppressing wrongdoing and in sustaining justice and order in people's dealings with each other. It urges making sure that public services are available to all and not just to those who can afford them. Finally, it approves a range of government initiatives to assist the disadvantaged, however physically, socially, intellectually, or psychologically impaired, as a way of sharing the benefits of the economy. Restrictive in some sense of liberty, it is nevertheless effective in widening the scope of freedom's economic benefits. In short, liberty, and equality as social values must be balanced, mutually interacting, and of common concern to be effective.

That is to say that a sense of fraternity and community highlights the fact that cooperation and collaboration are of the essence of business and of the economic process. Without minimizing in any way the motive force of self-interested gain seeking, Fraternity deplores the conflicts that inevitably arise and sees a disposition to share generously as the way not only to resolve disputes but to avoid them. Moreover, it knows that generosity both stimulates freedom and counteracts government's itching to intervene in the economy. It especially perceives all economic actors, however subordinate or dominant their functions, as human persons with natures, careers, and destinies that transcend their economic goals. Therefore, just as the blending of competitive efficiency, government's moderating mediation, and the sharing of efforts and benefits makes for a prospering economy, so it in turn contributes to the general Common Good.

Finally, there is no permanent solution to the disharmonies, inconsistencies, and imbalances among a person's and a people's roles and relationships. One's needs, relations, resources, abilities, and values change constantly. All impact not only on society, polity, and economy but also on the principles by which the economy is organized and run. There is, therefore, no definitive formula to a correct and lasting resolution of the economy's failures and of the shortcomings of the people who run it. At best, only guidelines are available on how attitudes, practices, and policies can produce a more reasonable and human life together. But the most necessary is the will to treat one's family, relatives, friends, associates, coworkers, and fellow citizens as economic persons.

REFERENCES

Allport, Gordon W. *Pattern and Growth in Personality*. New York: Holt, 1965.

Danner, Peter L. "Personalism and the Common Good." *The Social Economics of Human Material Need*. Edited by J. B. Davis and E. J. O'Boyle. Carbondale, Ill.:Southern Illinois University Press, 1994.

Dempsey, Bernard W., S. J. *The Functional Economy: The Bases of Economic Organization*. Englewood Cliffs, N.J.: Prentice Hall, 1958.

Marx, Karl. *Capital*. Translated by S. Moore and E. Aveling and edited by Friedrich Engels. Great Books of the Western World Series edited by Robert Maynard Hutchins. Chicago: Encyclopedia Britannica, 1952.

Mounier, Emmanuel. *Personalism*. Translated by Phillip Mairet. South Bend, Ind.: University of Notre Dame Press, 1952.

Myrdal, Gunnar. *An American Dilemma: The Negro Problem and Modern Democracy*. New York: Harper & Row, 1944.

Scheler, Max. *Formalism in Ethics and Non-Formal Ethics of Value: A New Attempt Toward the Foundation of an Ethical Personalism*. Translated by M. Frings and R. Funk. Evanston, Ill.: Northwestern University Press, 1973.

Scruton, Roger. *The Aesthetics of Architecture*. Princeton, N.J.: Princeton University Press, 1979.

Walton, Clarence, ed. *The Ethics of Corporate Conduct*. Englewood Cliffs, N.J.: Prentice Hall, 1977.

Chapter Ten

Economic Persons in Action

The previous topics—scarcity pricing, economic valuing, competitive gain seeking, collaborating/sharing, and the economy's role in the Societal Common Good—all relate to three of the most basic issues of personalist economics. The first is the need and importance of distinguishing between economics as analysis (i.e., as science) and economics as doing (i.e., as praxis). Second, real and effective personal economic behavior results from melding differing principles of action. Third, economic persons as such must be motivated by self-interest and their acts can be judged both economically rational/irrational and morally good/bad. This account, therefore, would be incomplete unless it spoke to these issues, which the complexity of economic thought, the person's body/spirit nature and economic needs and wants pose for the economic person's acting both rationally and morally.

ANALYSIS AND PRAXIS

The voice of wisdom urges against discussing or even mentioning the differences between economics as analysis and economics as praxis, since the two necessarily blend into each other in real life. Nevertheless, the issue must be addressed to avoid later confusion. The problem, of course, is that economics as science is dealing not with neutrons or chemicals but with real, living people, who both analyze economic behavior and engage in that behavior themselves. Further, since economic persons are infinitely varied by gender, age, health, race, culture, mental acuity, and politics and differ in ambitions and aspirations, they diverge greatly in their economic possibilities. Thus every economic act of any person is absolutely unique, but all the economic acts of all persons are so blended together that the economy at any one moment can

149

be considered as a whole, as the cumulative yet constantly changing product of innumerable personal acts. Gathering and collating all of these acts is itself a great and continuous undertaking because it means that at any particular moment the economy can be, and is, analyzed as such by professional economists, be they academic, business, or government.

That analysis must necessarily be expressed in quantitative, empirical, and almost physical terms—tendencies, drives, pressures, rates of change, ratios, or slowdowns —and as performed by abstract agents—management, labor, markets, Wall Street, the "Fed," and so on. Whichever ways these professional analyses go, they will generate further changes so that the economy is really in constant flux, sometimes slower, sometimes faster. The result is that the economic person, the real agent of economic acts, becomes in those analyses a faceless economic calculator, losing almost all personality. This is true whether he or she is in some cases moved by greed, in others by desperate poverty, by dishonesty, or by charity. Whichever, economic analysis simply records the facts of the act, abstracting from any and all personal implications.

But while the economic agent may thus seem to lose economic personality, he or she has not lost personal responsibility. Economics as science may seem as personless as archeology or physics, the economic person, however, as embodied spirit and thus needing and wanting material things, is still a moral being. In acting on these needs and wants, the economic person nevertheless transcends the merely material, is ordained to relate to and interact with other persons, must live in an ordered and lawful social order, and is destined for a life beyond this life. All such implies moral roles whose rights and obligations require a different science that might be called economic morality, moral principles as relating to economic actions. That is, it yields principles for judging economic acts as right or wrong in distinction from economic science's judgments as rational or irrational. Thus the two analyses may seem at times to be at loggerheads with each other: what looks economically rational may not be moral, and vice versa. But despite seeming to clash in the give and take of ordinary living, they cannot contradict. The solution is for each science to respect the other's legitimacy, to hold to the need for each and their respective rationalities, and then gradually to work out the seeming contrarieties.

TRINITARIAN REALISM AND RELATIONS

The necessary blending of economic rationality and economic morality is but another case exemplifying that all of human reality is trinitarian and triangular, that is, a relating and blending of two differences and contraries that, instead of canceling each other, form a third essentially higher reality. (Here it is important to recall the distinction between contraries and contradictions. Contradictions, up/down, cancel each other; if one is true, the other cannot be. Contraries differ but do not deny each other—blue is not yellow—but they can be blended to form green. Contradictions destroy; contraries create.) Spirit and body, however, are not contradictions. They differ but can be, and in fact are, blended in the human person.

The most apposite analogy is the triangle: where two sides are joined at a right or larger angle, the square on the third side is equal to or greater than the sum of the squares on the other two sides. For examples in the physical universe, the interaction of rock and water makes soil; soil and seeds produce plants; plants and solar power yield a harvest. The blending of contraries always has the potential of generating a synergy which can produce something superior to both.

Regarding the human person, the matter/spirit integration is so dynamic that the voice, sound, symbol, quantifying and moving systems, and the incalculable variety of structures and processes which humans have created over the millennia have totally differentiated them from all other animals. But of all the trinitarian systems contributing to humanity's growth and progress, the most basic is the female/male nexus, resulting from their mutual attraction as differently embodied spirits. Beyond simply generating children this union has established a third and most creative society: the human family as the energizer and support of spiritual, cultural, social, and economic institutions.

Paralleling this in importance is the triangular process of human knowing. This is a blending of two fundamental ways: the empirical/inductive, which is largely the method of economic science, and the intuitive/deductive, the way of moral reasoning. The first is the method of factual observation, data organization, and correlation into pragmatic principles. The second proceeds from time-honored ways of thinking, feeling, and acting, from insights into the nature and essence of human beings and their universal convictions. From these initial premises are drawn principle of conduct. The contrast between the empirical and intuitive is the cause of dispute between science and morality, but it can and does generate a deeper understanding of the nature and conduct of the human person. Science has cleared up much false opinions about persons, animals, and things, but in doing so it has also enhanced people's intuition into their own natures.

All this expresses the basic insight of a personalist philosophy that the human person is both unique and related to everyone else, is both self-knowing and other-cultivating, and must, therefore, act both individually and socially.

Chapter Ten

This is no less true of economic actions even though economic theory can abstract from this and consider only the material content of acts—prices paid, products sold, hours worked, and interest earned—and analyze and predict their effects. But every economic act, nevertheless, is social, involving and affecting others, and hence its agent is both social and individual and his or her act both economic and moral. Because it is a personal act, however, the economic person must address the problem of melding economic and personalist insights into an effective economic morality.

The Econo-Moral Meld

In what follows, the chapter will address six pairs of contraries: material reality/embodied spirit; wanting/needing; economic values/personal values; gaining/dealing; self-interest/collaborating; economy's organizing principles/democracy's social values. The first treats the problem of the person's role in the universe and the last five roughly parallel the subjects of chapters 5 through 9.

The first and obvious fact of human reality is the spirit's involvement in the material universe, itself a wonderful abode so plentifully supplied with still largely untapped resources and powers. In response to this, the spirit's innate drives to know more clearly and universally, to love more deeply, and to enjoy more extensively has created a vast array of goods and services which first must be fashioned and formed for human use and are, consequently, called 'scarce' but in fact must be 'priced.'

That refers to a special motivating and exchange instrument: really a cognitive construct called price, a universal means for evaluating products and services in terms of one generally accepted good called 'money,' be it fishhooks, perhaps, in tribal societies or gold in more advanced societies or, as today, economic credit. As such, pricing is fundamental to that vast and seething process called the economy by which means the human spirit, by directing its powers and skills to this planet, has over the last five millennia transformed human living and habitation beyond what human beings could imagine in the prior thousands of millennia.

Ironically, however, that utopian promise has never been realized fully but only in a flawed form. This is so not because of the pricing system itself but because of the evils infecting its use, specifically in nourishing greed, sensuality, and envy. As always moral failure is not owing to economic techniques but to human culpability. Illustrating this is the most fundamental and wiliest issue to handle, that of relating human wanting to needing. How fundamental this relation is requires one only to consider that, as embodied spirit, the economic person needs material goods and, therefore, has to want them.

Needing and Wanting

There are four English words relevant here: 'lack' as a general term, that something desirable is missing; 'necessity,' referring to something or a state for which there is no substitute; 'need,' the lack of something essential; and 'want,' something a person intends or hopes to acquire. Only the last two terms are sufficient for analysis here: needing is the state of lacking something essential for survival like food, shelter, or medical service, for personal growth like education, for economic exchanging like money, and for social and political living like language, writing, property, or laws. Thus need, as things natural to personal well-being, is generic, and need itself refers only to the state of lacking and does not imply acts to remedy the situation. Want, on the other hand, does imply an intention and actual effort to acquire a specific product or service among those able to minister to the need. Every economic act, therefore, is an act of wanting, whether the thing wanted is needed, desirable, beneficial, or not. Needing and wanting, consequently, range into all aspects of human action. Here only the economic will be considered.

The manifest nexus between the two contraries is the economic person, who as embodied spirit has not only basic survival needs but social, cultural, political, and economic needs consistent with one's changing roles in society and one's destiny as a person. Needs, therefore, are more important in elevating one's wanting and more fundamental in relating the person, in constant process of physical and spiritual change, to material goods and services. But wanting is more effective in moving a person to get a specific thing to satisfy real or imagined need. Wanting, since it effects the transfer and acquisition of material things, is empirical and measurable, while needing is at most intentional only. Nevertheless the two exist in dynamic tension; needs generate wants, but often wants can become needs or quasi needs.

The usual right moral order is that needing should direct wanting although wanting can become so habitual and addictive as to seem a need: occasional drug use becomes addiction or love for another becomes a passion to please. More frequently, greed, emulation, invidiousness, and so on—'consumerism' as it is called—can so pervert persons' needing as to transform their wanting into uncontrolled impulses even despite others' real needs. On the other hand, a clear understanding of what one needs for living, for one's vocation, and for fulfilling one's social, economic, and political obligations not only uses goods and services more efficiently but tends to enhance the pleasure from nonessential want satisfactions. Thus moderating one's needing and especially one's wanting, not only in line with common sense but moreso in view of others' more desperate needs, is by all odds the most fundamental issue in economic morality. The following triangular relations illustrates this further and more specifically.

Values, Gain, Collaboration, Common Good

The first such is to examine how economic valuing relates to personal (moral) valuing, the link being that the economic person is morally responsible for his or her final destiny and must rely on the products and the services the economy yields. Thus persons must both fashion their ruling values and value hierarchies, ordering them according to their permanence, basis, essence, and integrity, and also weigh the cost and utility of the material contents of the values. In this pragmatic sense, moral and economic values are joined in concrete actions.

As stated earlier, some of the most valued goods are priceless: a sunset, a baby's smile, memories of a friend. Although some pricing may be involved even here, almost everything else for sure is priced. Most things are valued both for their use value as product or service and as means to a more expensive good. But high moral value is no guarantee of high exchange (economic) value. Things and people desired for their violence, dishonesty, and sensuality may command high prices and may generate profitable markets. This is usually so because costs are so high and supply limited. (Where such is commonplace or becomes standard, the economy is a disaster.) In short, basic social and moral values lay an essential foundation both for sound markets and for economic growth and prosperity.

This seems, however, to go against the ingrained principle of economic self-interest, to seek gain in every economic act. But the economy's growth and personal gain seeking cannot be at odds, since economic growth is but the sum of individual gains. The reason is that dealing as involving exchange with other gain seekers is the only way to realize a net social gain. (This is even true of the self-employed who must surrender the benefit from one task to get more benefit from another, e.g,. put off cutting wood to till a field.) As a rational economic calculator, a person can gain from exchange only by allowing another to deal, to gain from the exchange also. In this, each plays the diminishing marginal utility game, that more of anything, even money, has decreasing use value but can be made more profitable by exchanging it for other wanted but less plentiful goods.

Thus, dealing fairly with others even while competing for gain becomes the means for disseminating gain throughout the economy, for spurring trade and thereby economic growth. Consequently, economic justice, respecting others' rights and giving all exchanging parties their due, is also fundamental to economic growth. As chapter 8 demonstrated, theft and fraud not only destroy values but also kill initiative by amassing wealth in the hands of the few. On the other hand, generosity to those in need can be most economically productive when it does not encourage dependence but rather arouses incentive as shown in chapter 7. All in all, economic growth must be shared to be judged morally good.

Although sharing also seems to reject the economic principle of self-interest, economic acts, even though competitive as well as self-interested, are *collaborative*. Economic agents are both and simultaneously wanter and worker. A person can get what he or she wants only by joining others in providing what other people want. Innovating, investing, producing, and trading are all collaborative actions, that is, persons need and must associate with others to make the economy go and grow. (Even Robinson Crusoe used tools and techniques others developed and had Friday to help him.) That is, the nexus between self-interest and cooperation is an essential element of human sociality. People are no less related by birth, interests, and activities than they are by concern about the economy's prosperity and their participation in it. In short, collaboration always fructifies self-interest.

This blending of self-concern and other-relating also generates true community, here seen as an internal organizing principle of economic institutions. Essential to this is accepting others, their talents, and self-interests as integral to the functioning of the organization. It includes a sense of generosity in supplementing others' shortcomings and beyond this in sharing one's economic well-being with those in need. Hence, it takes generosity to another dimension of communal and fraternal concern.

All in all, this seminal fusing of differences—material resources and embodied spirit; wants and needs; moral values and economic values; gain seeking and competitive dealing; self-interest and collaborative sharing—leads to the interactive blending of personalist social, political, and economic undertakings into the *social common good*. The three social values endemic to democracy—or to any truly humanistic government—liberty, equality, and fraternity manifest the same triangularity in that only from a mutually confirming and restraining liberty and equality can a true sense of fraternity arise. This last, in turn, ideally fixes the three into a dynamic trilogy of social, political, and economic interaction. More specifically to the economy, the three values inspire and blend the basic economic principles of organization—competition, government mediation, and cooperation in innovating, producing, and trading—so as to generate a fruitful and widely beneficent economy.

All the preceding analyses come down to seeing how morality and economics, both equally valid sciences of human behavior, fit together. The answer, of course, is that the subjects of both are *economic persons*, some of the analyses are concerned about how this system works and others what moral principles apply. But all persons are economic doers and agents, developing and using the assets and forces of material nature and by the same means achieving a final destiny. Thus moral and economic patterns of behavior are analogous.

Economic rationality requires a *prudence* in choosing one good over another. Risk-taking about markets, pricing, jobs, investment, and business strategy is a form of *courage*. Trading and the rationale of prices, expenses, and costs impose an economic *moderation*. *Justice*, at least in sharing gain with collaborators, employees, and exchange partners, is essential because of the social nature of economics and business.

Rational choice must be made from a complex of competing and complementary wants, of many economic persons participating in production and exchange for the sake of gain and to satisfy present wants against future needs. Balancing all these wants and aspirations is of the essence and forms the texture of the *econo-moral meld*. Blending moral convictions and economic rationality makes for the most economic common sense.

While such blending of contraries enriches the texture of the economic person and his or her life and actions, the more basic difficulty still arises from the need to control one's natural self-interest.

SELF-INTEREST

Self-interest presents problems both from an economic and a personalist perspective. First, all conscious and intentional acts are self-interested because what a person intends is always in line with the basic law of human nature, to seek what is seen as good and to avoid what is bad. That is a person's most fundamental concern or interest. Self-interest, therefore, is also necessary for a personalist morality, based as it is on self-knowing, self-judging, self-valuing, and ultimately seeking one's personal good. It is also inherent in the economic act. Needing and wanting economic goods or services, buying and selling, competing for gain and cooperating as required in every economic function, all manifest self-interest. The economic person is necessarily self-interested. The problems this poses may be suggested by looking at the results of self-interest on a larger palette.

Self-Interest in Action

National self-interest, which is much like individual self-interest written large, has been the basic cause of two centuries plus of the bloodiest wars in human history. Now include territorial aggressions; class, national, and racial revolutions; tribal, ethnic, and religious purgings; and the extermination of political dissidents and other outcasts. Then add to these public holocausts the sad record of private killings: terrorism, assassinations, gang warfare, traffic deaths, domestic fatalities, and not least of all, millions of private and state-mandated abortions. All this public and private mayhem has forced millions of people to risk unimaginable suffering in fleeing their homelands, all in the name of national self-interest.

Against this spectacle of human brutality the last two centuries yield another picture of a health-care profession almost doubling peoples' life expectancy; agricultural progress wiping out starvation, if allowed to; industries producing adequate housing and clothing for all; scientific research constantly expanding persons' understanding of themselves as well as the potencies and resources not only of this earth but of the cosmos; and finally, travel and communication bringing all parts of the world into daily contact. Never before have peoples been made more aware of their differences as well as their similarities.

While the story of the century's aggression, destruction, and killing is relieved by innumerable acts of heroism and self-sacrifice, its most publicized records are accounts of personal, class, religious, racial, and chauvinistic quarrels, hatreds, and cruelty. In other words, they testify to complete disregard for the personhood of peoples who differ from the predominant ethnic heritage, deviate from the prevailing culture, oppose the powers that be, or block one's wants. While a few may openly oppose such injustice or quietly help the outcasts and disenfranchised, some people would take advantage of such conditions and most would judge it best simply to tolerate them.

Something the same happens in economic matters. Slash-and-burn agriculture prevails where not prevented, as do sweatshops, child labor, monopolistic pricing, dishonest investing, and shoddy merchandising. While the modern industrial economy may be beneficent in extending life and making it more comfortable and livable, there is little reason to think that those who run some part of or otherwise engage in the economic process are any more or less selfish or altruistic than those who control or are engaged in government, the arts, or education. While the few have, often selfishly, acquired much more than most, many, on the other hand, live frugally so as to help others. Even more telling are national and international responses to personal tragedies or natural disasters. All told, *economic self-interest* presents a mixed but disturbing picture.

Future historians, assessing the above, may well ponder calling the twentieth century another Dark Age like a sixth or ninth century in Western civilization or a giant leap forward for humanity toward international comity and oversight. The grotesque incongruity between the beneficent and baleful pictures of the century is startling. But even more amazing is that both patterns of conduct were motivated mainly by national and personal self-interests. All suggest that self-interest as seeking the good, as one sees it, is a force inherent in all of life and is, consequently, more complex than the naked selfishness many, including innumerable economic theorists, assume that it is. For sure self-interest, personal interest, and selfishness could stand closer scrutiny.

Self-Interest and Selfishness

What people are concerned about or interested in is some good they seek or some evil they would avoid. Thus all human acts in this basic sense are self-interested. But not all are selfish. An act done to benefit another or some others or to ward off an evil may be of some benefit to one's self or may be entirely altruistic, that is, of benefit to another even at cost to one's self. This last occurs when someone has taken a personal interest in another's well being. (For example, Uncle Henry has taken a *personal interest* in Cousin Jake's acting career as if it were his own and at cost to himself.) Between selfishness and such pure altruism are many gradations of self-interest and considerations of others' good. The same holds for economic acts, all with varying self-interests. In most the buyer is quite willing for the seller to realize some benefit and vice versa. There may be various elements of cheating and deception, but both buyer and seller must respect the other's self-interest in a general way.

Also beyond the nature of the act itself is the *purpose* for which the act is done and who will *benefit* or be *harmed*. For example, a teen gang leader and a policeman may each buy a revolver, each act producing initially the same economic effect, the sale of an economic good, the seller realizing a profit, and each acquiring a desired property. But each intends quite different uses: the former to steal and kill, the latter to protect life and property. The differing purposes then convert the self-interest of one into selfishness and of the other into altruism. Similarly the potential future economic effect of the former will be harmful and of the latter beneficial. The purpose for acting, of course, may not be so clearly differentiated. For example, a woman may shop for her family and include a delicacy for herself. Nevertheless, *purpose* as the reason for the act, the goal sought, or the beneficiary helped is the first and most important criterion in judging self-interest.

Next, self-interest is very much conditioned by what is the object sought or avoided, specifically whether it is material or spiritual (here meaning nonmaterial and not necessarily moral). Products of the mind, heart, and imagination, expressed in words, sounds, movements, colors, and so on, are intended for others and in this sense, even though otherwise immoral, are altruistic. Such become public property in that songs may be sung privately, poems recited, and dancing imitated without let or leave. Where copyrights are ignored or when terminated, such spiritual goods belong to everyone.

Most sport events are like this and are free to be enjoyed. Organized contests, especially major ones, however, are in a different category. While generally gaudy commercial events, parading promoters' and players' passion for cold cash, they still partake of the nature of spiritual goods. As displays of skills and purpose for an audience to enjoy, they have been touted in all societies throughout history as manifesting institutional, provincial, or national glory or gloom.

But getting, owning, using, and disposing of physical goods, as well as materialized spiritual goods like a book, can and do more clearly present problems of economic self-interest becoming selfish. Because persons as *embodied* spirits need physical goods for their well-being and conduct and because such goods, as products of human skill and work, are much desired but scarce, they inevitably become objects of contention and conflict. Thus ownership rights must be defined and protected with, if need be, the appropriate use of force. Moreover, since persons are both unique and bound to each other, rights to economic goods must be seen and sanctioned in their social setting. This, therefore, implies the *right to possess*, to keep, and to use material goods and the *right to dispossess* oneself of them. That is, if a person is to own and not be owned by physical goods, he or she must be able to sell them, to give them away, or to discard them, harming no one. In none of this is self-interest inherently selfish.

On the other hand, being realistic admits that selfishness taints the self-interest of most people, rich and poor alike. It acknowledges that accumulating wealth by any means possible, and regardless of injustice to others, can damage the economy itself beyond the initial hurt to people. Widespread social evils like wage slavery, fraud, embezzling, stealing, and all the ways people intend to gain wealth at the expense of others beyond destroying social relations, impairs how the economy functions. A universally selfish self-interest, if such would be true of any society, would ruin its economy, since no one could trust anyone else.

Quite otherwise, a fundamental altruism is necessary to make the economy go. For the most part people satisfy their own needs and wants by aiding others to satisfy theirs. Since the right to earn gives the right to dispose, wealth acquired in money form will be exchanged for other goods. It is this right-foot/left-foot alternation of earning/owning and selling/buying that drives the economy. Nothing more so than this manifests the inherent individual/social reality of the human person in his or her economic actions and relations.

Consequently, while every economic act is and must be self-interested, the degree of selfishness and/or altruism motivating the act will be defined by the very purpose and nature of the act, that is, the nature of the object sought and the reason why sought. Therefore, these brief philosophic comments can, in turn, serve to critique the current scene in a general way.

To control selfish self-interests, most people would agree that the state as guardian of the Common Good, including the economy, should have a preponderance of force. This, for sure, presents a great temptation to use it for the state's own economic purposes—or worse, the rulers' ends. Such is a never-ending possibility and needs constant vigilance. Taken to extremes, government power can become might over right: the might of superpowers over the right to national independence; the might of the state over the rights of citizens, the might of the powerful or political favorites over the rights of the general public.

By contrast business and economic self-interest does not in itself have the same potential to harm others. The power driving it is not force or fear but desires for gain by way of servicing the needs and wants of others. The two most obvious facts about wealth as monetary purchasing power are that it is desired and envied. But it must be surrendered to get what one wants, and to increase it one must consult others' interests and wants, lending it at interest or investing it as working capital to generate production and trade. This is not to deny that those possessing much money are better able to realize their self-interest even by taking advantage of others' ignorance and fear. Nor does it assert that humans in their economic and business roles are more benevolent than in their roles as citizens, soldiers, and public officials. Exchangeability, if seen as a "peddler principle," may mean that all is for sale: virtue, friendship, honor, and justice. But it affirms that exploiting one's power to purchase is inherently linked to others' desires. Indeed it urges considering how a more benevolent self-interest could advance one's own as well as others' well-being, by seeing and dealing with them as persons.

There can be no doubt that an embedded selfishness, cruelty, prejudice, and hatred can so divide one person from another, one people from another, and one nation from another that one group treats the other as mere means to their own public or personal good, denying their basic dignity as persons. On the other hand, the humanitarianism that is universally extolled as concern for others' well being may also be motivated by income expectations. Civil servants, researchers, doctors, pastors, teachers, and others, all rightly praised for efforts to help others, should be able to gain a living from their humanitarian efforts. For some this might be modest but for others quite handsome. In this respect they are acting the same as the less praised, who trade on the needs and wants of people. In sum, personal self-interest is not in and of itself rooted in selfishness, thus refuting Hobbes's dictum that people prey like wolves on each other. But the possibility is always there.

From this a further possible conclusion arises that economic and moral principles, while differing and perhaps seemingly contradictory, can and should be joined in guiding personal economic interests. The shortest and most pointed reason for affirming this is that each human person is simultaneously economic and moral agent. As embodied, the economic person can survive and work out his or her destiny only by using the resources and powers of the material universe and by converting them into useful forms in collaboration with other persons. As self-knowing and self-judging spirits, persons use material means and objects not just as such but to express their thought and feelings, to bond with others, and to seek a reality beyond the present. All of this confirms that self-interest is not a monogenetic selfishness but reflects the duality of body and spirit, a blending of differences to form the 'trinitarian' human person and agent. That is, the economic person, as a material/spiritual composite, is more intriguing, fascinating, and creative than its components considered separately.

The real problem, therefore, by way of analyzing economic morality lies in not just imposing some simplistic principle like selfish self-interest to explain economic conduct but in not accepting the fact, apparent from daily experience, that economic persons are complex beings and their actions the melding of contrary principles. In sum, it is clear throughout this study that economics is not a moral science in a strict sense. Nor is it an *immoral science*, needing such immoral principles as selfishness, injustice, or deceit to function. Its dicta and principles apply only to persons' physical and temporal ends. But since production, exchange, and pricing are needed to effect most physical acts, most economists hold that exchange and use values and the functioning of prices, markets, and trade-offs create a necessary, though mediatory, process by which human purposes are achieved and thus implicitly moral values espoused. Conversely, since economic persons as embodied spirits can achieve their ultimate purposes and goals only by material means, all physical acts, including the economic, affect their relations with others, influence their value espousals, and help to realize their dramas and destinies as persons. Therefore, a personalist perspective on those self-aware, social, valuing, communal, and transcendent impulses of human persons affirms the physical constraints and limitations on their transpersonal aspirations.

In short, economics, as most economists and other scholars have maintained, is not only essential for making a living but for living itself. The economic person as agent in action is not only individual but social, wanting wealth but necessarily sharing it, pricing products and services but valuing them, using others yet needing and often committed to them, self-interested yet bonded to the Societal Common Good.

Index

About the Author

Peter L. Danner is professor emeritus, economics, at Marquette University where he has taught for a quarter century. *The Economic Person: Acting and Analyzing* is his third book and, like the previous two—*An Ethics for the Affluent* and *Getting and Spending*—is in the area of ethics and philosophy. The same is true for most of his articles, published in collections such as *The Social Economics of Human Material Need* and *Social Economics: Premises, Findings, and Policies*, and in reviews such as *Thought, Ethics, Review of Social Economy, International Review of Social Economy*, and *Forum for Social Economy*.